M000034520

RHYMING WITH
JESUS

It takes a daily walk to sound like Jesus!

T R A C I   B R I T T

ISBN 978-1-0980-3747-5 (paperback)
ISBN 978-1-0980-3748-2 (hardcover)
ISBN 978-1-0980-3749-9 (digital)

Copyright © 2020 by Traci Britt

All rights reserved. No part of this publication may be reproduced, distributed, or transmitted in any form or by any means, including photocopying, recording, or other electronic or mechanical methods without the prior written permission of the publisher. For permission requests, solicit the publisher via the address below.

Christian Faith Publishing, Inc.
832 Park Avenue
Meadville, PA 16335
www.christianfaithpublishing.com

Scripture taken from the Holy Bible, *New International Version,* ® NIV. ® Copyright © 1973, 1978, 1984 by Biblica, Inc.™ Used by permission of Zondervan. All rights reserved worldwide. www.zondervan.com.

Printed in the United States of America

To: _____

From: _____

JANUARY 1

God did not promise
A trouble-free life
Yet that He would
Help us through our strife

Pray and seek God
When you begin your day
He will be with you
Every step of the way

The Lord is good to those whose hope is in him,
to the one who seeks him;
Lamentations 3:25

"I have told you these things, so that in me you
may have peace. In this world you will have trou-
ble. But take heart! I have overcome the world."
John 16:33

If any of you lacks wisdom, he should ask God,
who gives generously to all without finding fault,
and it will be given to him.
James 1:5

JANUARY 2

To know Jesus
Is to be set free
For through Jesus Christ
Death no longer holds me

Eternal life I was given
When Jesus came into my heart
And neither death nor sin
Could ever make Him depart

For I am convinced that neither death nor life, neither angels nor demons, neither the present nor the future, nor any powers, neither height nor depth, nor anything else in all creation, will be able to separate us from the love of God that is in Christ Jesus our Lord.

Romans 8:38–39

I give them eternal life, and they shall never perish; no one can snatch them out of my hand.

John 10:28

but it has now been revealed through the appearing of our Savior, Christ Jesus, who has destroyed death and has brought life and immortality to light through the gospel.

2 Timothy 1:10

JANUARY 3

When my cup is empty
I still do not fear
I know our God
Is always right here

I lift up my hands
And to Him I pray
For He refills my cup
Each and every day

Then Jesus declared, "I am the bread of life. He
who comes to me will never go hungry, and he
who believes in me will never be thirsty.
John 6:35

Lord, you have assigned me my portion and my
cup; you have made my lot secure.
Psalm 16:5

May the God of hope fill you with all joy and
peace as you trust in him, so that you may over-
flow with hope by the power of the Holy Spirit.
Romans 15:13

JANUARY 4

No matter what you're going through
Regardless of where you have been
Jesus loves and forgives you
It doesn't matter what type of sin

You are worthy
Of His mercy and grace
Give your heart to Jesus
For your eternal place

for all have sinned and fall short of the glory of God, and are justified freely by his grace through the redemption that came by Christ Jesus.
Romans 3:23–24

But because of his great love for us, God, who is rich in mercy, made us alive with Christ even when we were dead in transgressions—it is by grace you have been saved.
Ephesians 2:4–5

For the grace of God that brings salvation has appeared to all men.
Titus 2:11

JANUARY 5

What a glorious day
As I rise and shine
My heart filled with happiness
Knowing You are mine

Mold me and shape me
Flowing with joy
I am like a child
With a new toy

Therefore, whoever humbles himself like this child is the greatest in the kingdom of heaven.
Matthew 18:4

Like newborn babies, crave pure spiritual milk, so that by it you may grow up in your salvation,
1 Peter 2:2

I have told you this so that my joy may be in you and that your joy may be complete.
John 15:11

JANUARY 6

When I am empty
I turn to the Lord
I lift up His praise
And I thirst no more

He knows my needs
Before I even speak
For my daily bread
It is Jesus I seek

They all ate the same spiritual food and drank the same spiritual drink; for they drank from the spiritual rock that accompanied them, and that rock was Christ.
                    1 Corinthians 10:3–4

Before a word is on my tongue you know it completely, O Lord.
                    Psalm 139:4

Do not be like them, for your Father knows what you need before you ask him.
                    Matthew 6:8

JANUARY 7

I am not perfect
And I don't have to be
Because God sent His only son
To die for you and me

What He asks in return
Is to let Him in your heart
Put Him first each day
In everything let Him be a part

"For God so loved the world that he gave his one
and only Son, that whoever believes in him shall
not perish but have eternal life.
John 3:16

Then he called the crowd to him along with his
disciples and said: "If anyone would come after
me, he must deny himself and take up his cross
and follow me.
Mark 8:34

in all your ways acknowledge him, and he will
make your paths straight.
Proverbs 3:6

JANUARY 8

Remember the sacrifice
Jesus made for you and me
Without His love for us
Where would we be

How can I help someone today
A sacrifice of myself
The love of Jesus does no good
If I keep it locked up on a shelf

And let us consider how we may spur one another
on toward love and good deeds.
Hebrews 10:24

Therefore, my brothers, be all the more eager to
make your calling and election sure. For if you
do these things, you will never fall, and you will
receive a rich welcome into the eternal kingdom
of our Lord and Savior Jesus Christ.
2 Peter 1:10–11

But God demonstrates his own love for us in this:
While we were still sinners, Christ died for us.
Romans 5:8

JANUARY 9

Just when I get ahead
It seems something goes wrong
More than a head above water
Is for what I long

I'm at a crossroads
In my mind
Do I give the devil room
No, I trust Jesus and know I'm fine

The Lord is good, a refuge in times of trouble.
He cares for those who trust in him,
Nahum 1:7

and do not give the devil a foothold.
Ephesians 4:27

A greedy man stirs up dissension, but he who
trusts in the Lord will prosper.
Proverbs 28:25

JANUARY 10

Some people just seem like
They are out to steal your joy
Only they can control
The intent of their ploy

Then it is in my hands
I must decide what to do
Do I return the favor
Or let Jesus shine through

Make every effort to live in peace with all men and to be holy; without holiness no one will see the Lord.

Hebrews 12:14

Do not repay evil with evil or insult with insult, but with blessing, because to this you were called so that you may inherit a blessing.

1 Peter 3:9

Make sure that nobody pays back wrong for wrong, but always try to be kind to each other and to everyone else.

1 Thessalonians 5:15

JANUARY 11

When I pray
Do I put God in a box
Or do I fully believe
Is that so unorthodox

Today I choose to grow
And I am going to fully believe
I pray in God's will
Not in what I perceive

But when he asks, he must believe and not doubt,
because he who doubts is like a wave of the sea,
blown and tossed by the wind.
James 1:6

Therefore I tell you, whatever you ask for in
prayer, believe that you have received it, and it
will be yours.
Mark 11:24

And the prayer offered in faith will make the sick
person well; the Lord will raise him up. If he has
sinned, he will be forgiven.
James 5:15

JANUARY 12

Build me up
As Your strong tower
So I will be ready
In that precious hour

Lord give me strength
Fill me with love
So I can humbly
Meet God above

So you also must be ready, because the Son of Man will come at an hour when you do not expect him.

Matthew 24:44

When these things begin to take place, stand up and lift up your heads, because your redemption is drawing near."

Luke 21:28

This calls for patient endurance on the part of the saints who obey God's commandments and remain faithful to Jesus.

Revelation 14:12

JANUARY 13

You never know
Whose life you may change
When you give in Christ
Whatever is in your range

It may be your time
Service, tithe or listening ear
Always do it in Christ
Keeping His love near

God is not unjust; he will not forget your work
and the love you have shown him as you have
helped his people and continue to help them.
Hebrews 6:10

Remember this: Whoever sows sparingly will also
reap sparingly, and whoever sows generously will
also reap generously.
2 Corinthians 9:6

He who is kind to the poor lends to the Lord,
and he will reward him for what he has done.
Proverbs 19:17

JANUARY 14

God is patient
And He is kind
Not wanting you to perish
Or be left behind

So live each day
In His glory and grace
Drawing closer to God
And His heavenly face

The Lord is not slow in keeping his promise, as some understand slowness. He is patient with you, not wanting anyone to perish, but everyone to come to repentance.

2 Peter 3:9

while we wait for the blessed hope—the glorious appearing of our great God and Savior, Jesus Christ,

Titus 2:13

Or do you show contempt for the riches of his kindness, tolerance and patience, not realizing that God's kindness leads you toward repentance?

Romans 2:4

JANUARY 15

The Lord blesses us each day
Either we see it or turn away
We stand in misery and frown
Or claim the glory of His crown

I choose to open my eyes
Not to fret over the how's and why's
Not following the ways of man
But to live this day in God's plan

And God is able to make all grace abound to you,
so that in all things at all times, having all that
you need, you will abound in every good work.
2 Corinthians 9:8

In his heart a man plans his course, but the Lord
determines his steps.
Proverbs 16:9

It is better to take refuge in the Lord than to trust
in man.
Psalm 118:8

JANUARY 16

God loves me
Regardless of my sin
Yet there is discipline
When I do it again and again

Discipline with love
Is what He gives
And the desire to be like Him
When I became His

But you, O Lord, are a compassionate and gracious God, slow to anger, abounding in love and faithfulness.

Psalm 86:15

because the Lord disciplines those he loves, as a father the son he delights in.

Proverbs 3:12

No discipline seems pleasant at the time, but painful. Later on, however, it produces a harvest of righteousness and peace for those who have been trained by it.

Hebrews 12:11

JANUARY 17

I live each day
Searching for the next big thing
But emptiness and desire
Is what that will bring

For true fulfillment
Comes from within my heart
And Jesus Christ
Is where that will start

Then he said to them, "Watch out! Be on your guard against all kinds of greed; a man's life does not consist in the abundance of his possessions."
Luke 12:15

My flesh and my heart may fail, but God is the strength of my heart and my portion forever.
Psalm 73:26

That if you confess with your mouth, "Jesus is Lord," and believe in your heart that God raised him from the dead, you will be saved.
Romans 10:9

JANUARY 18

I may stumble
And I may fall
I know my Lord and Savior
Is with me through it all

He gives me strength
Surrounding me with peace
In Him I find a love
I know will never cease

The Lord your God is with you, he is mighty to save. He will take great delight in you, he will quiet you with his love, he will rejoice over you with singing."

Zephaniah 3:17

Though you have not seen him, you love him; and even though you do not see him now, you believe in him and are filled with an inexpressible and glorious joy,

1 Peter 1:8

As it is written: "See, I lay in Zion a stone that causes men to stumble and a rock that makes them fall, and the one who trusts in him will never be put to shame."

Romans 9:33

JANUARY 19

I am worthy
No matter how much I fall
Jesus is there with me
He loves me through it all

He takes away my fears
And puts my heart at ease
Mercy and grace abound
And brings me to my knees

For I know the plans I have for you," declares the Lord, "plans to prosper you and not to harm you, plans to give you hope and a future.
Jeremiah 29:11

But he gives us more grace. That is why Scripture says: "God opposes the proud but gives grace to the humble."
James 4:6

So do not fear, for I am with you; do not be dismayed, for I am your God. I will strengthen you and help you; I will uphold you with my righteous right hand.
Isaiah 41:10

JANUARY 20

As I am living
In this world day to day
I need to be mindful
Of which way I sway

For I am here
To influence others for God
Not the other way around
And follow where men trod

Therefore this is what the Lord says: "If you repent, I will restore you that you may serve me; if you utter worthy, not worthless, words, you will be my spokesman. Let this people turn to you, but you must not turn to them.
Jeremiah 15:19

And whatever you do, whether in word or deed, do it all in the name of the Lord Jesus, giving thanks to God the Father through him.
Colossians 3:17

Stay away from a foolish man, for you will not find knowledge on his lips.
Proverbs 14:7

JANUARY 21

Who am I
What do people see
As I go through my day
Do people see You in me

Are You in my daily walk
Can they see You in my smile
Do they look into my eyes
Seeing You all the while

"I am the true vine, and my Father is the gardener.
John 15:1

Follow my example, as I follow the example of Christ.
1 Corinthians 11:1

And over all these virtues put on love, which binds them all together in perfect unity.
Colossians 3:14

JANUARY 22

It doesn't take much
For Satan to grab hold
He doesn't care the pain or cost
Or how young or old

So put on your armor
At the beginning of each day
Lift up the Lord our God
And Satan will not stay

Put on the full armor of God so that you can take
your stand against the devil's schemes.
Ephesians 6:11

Submit yourselves, then, to God. Resist the devil,
and he will flee from you.
James 4:7

The God of peace will soon crush Satan under
your feet. The grace of our Lord Jesus be with
you.
Romans 16:20

Plant your faith
In the Lord above
And He will carry you
Like the wings of a dove

Stay strong and true
Keep your feet on the ground
Nothing better than Him
Can there be found

"But blessed is the man who trusts in the Lord, whose confidence is in him. He will be like a tree planted by the water that sends out its roots by the stream. It does not fear when heat comes; its leaves are always green. It has no worries in a year of drought and never fails to bear fruit."
Jeremiah 17:7–8

rooted and built up in him, strengthened in the faith as you were taught, and overflowing with thankfulness.

Colossians 2:7

planted in the house of the Lord, they will flourish in the courts of our God.

Psalm 92:13

JANUARY 24

If He can make the blind to see
And cure a leper's spots
Then I can surely trust Him
With any problem that I've got

For nothing in this world
Is too big or too small
Bring it all to Him in prayer
He will be there through it all

Such confidence as this is ours through Christ before God.

2 Corinthians 3:4

So do not fear, for I am with you; do not be dismayed, for I am your God. I will strengthen you and help you; I will uphold you with my righteous right hand.

Isaiah 41:10

Once more Jesus put his hands on the man's eyes. Then his eyes were opened, his sight was restored, and he saw everything clearly.

Mark 8:25

JANUARY 25

Do I live my life
Like tomorrow may never come
What is my legacy
Have I touched anyone

Do I leave a great fortune
To be squandered on earth
Or a desire to love Jesus
And to live up to Your worth

But the fruit of the Spirit is love, joy, peace, patience, kindness, goodness, faithfulness, gentleness and self-control. Against such things there is no law.

Galatians 5:22–23

A good man leaves an inheritance for his children's children, but a sinner's wealth is stored up for the righteous.

Proverbs 13:22

One generation will commend your works to another; they will tell of your mighty acts.

Psalm 145:4

JANUARY 26

The wind blows hardest
On the tallest tree
The more trials you face
The stronger you will be

God gives us strength
He is strong when we are weak
Always remember these truths
Let it be Him you seek

But he said to me, "My grace is sufficient for you, for my power is made perfect in weakness." Therefore I will boast all the more gladly about my weaknesses, so that Christ's power may rest on me.

2 Corinthians 12:9

He gives strength to the weary and increases the power of the weak.

Isaiah 40:29

God is our refuge and strength, an ever-present help in trouble.

Psalm 46:1

JANUARY 27

Anyone can hurt you
If you give them a chance
It may be a harsh word
Or a mean glance

Just know you are worthy
Of peace and of love
And your only judgement
Comes from God above

There is only one Lawgiver and Judge, the one who is able to save and destroy. But you—who are you to judge your neighbor?

James 4:12

For the Lord is our judge, the Lord is our lawgiver, the Lord is our king; it is he who will save us.

Isaiah 33:22

For we must all appear before the judgement seat of Christ, that each one may receive what is due him for the things done while in the body, whether good or bad.

2 Corinthians 5:10

JANUARY 28

The circumstances you are in
Do not determine who you are
Those plans are from Jesus
He can take you far

Don't let your surroundings
Set your pace
Let Jesus in your heart
And follow Him with grace

May God himself, the God of peace, sanctify you through and through. May your whole spirit, soul and body be kept blameless at the coming of our Lord Jesus Christ.

1 Thessalonians 5:23

Your word is a lamp to my feet and a light for my path.

Psalm 119:105

You need to persevere so that when you have done the will of God, you will receive what he has promised.

Hebrews 10:36

The joy of the Lord
Is my strength
He will be there for me
At any length

He is the first place
I will turn
Grace will abound
So that I may learn

The name of the Lord is a strong tower; the righteous run to it and are safe.

Proverbs 18:10

Nehemiah said, "Go and enjoy choice food and sweet drinks, and send some to those who have nothing prepared. This day is sacred to our Lord. Do not grieve, for the joy of the Lord is your strength."

Nehemiah 8:10

I will instruct you and teach you in the way you should go; I will counsel you and watch over you.

Psalm 32:8

JANUARY 30

It's okay to cry
And feel in dismay
Just don't turn away from God
And let those feelings stay

For He cares for you
He is compassionate and kind
Filling your heart with Jesus
Will leave your hurt behind

The Lord himself goes before you and will be
with you; he will never leave you nor forsake you.
Do not be afraid; do not be discouraged."
Deuteronomy 31:8

The righteous cry out, and the Lord hears them;
he delivers them from all their troubles.
Psalm 34:17

and the ransomed of the Lord will return. They
will enter Zion with singing; everlasting joy will
crown their heads. Gladness and joy will overtake
them, and sorrow and sighing will flee away.
Isaiah 35:10

JANUARY 31

I struggle with doing right
To those that do me wrong
Yet in my walk with Christ
This can't be my hearts song

For I can't control them
I can only account for me
And holding onto that anger
Isn't worth the fee

Bear with each other and forgive whatever griev-
ances you may have against one another. Forgive
as the Lord forgave you.

Colossians 3:13

For if you forgive men when they sin against you,
your heavenly Father will also forgive you. But if
you do not forgive men their sins, your Father
will not forgive your sins.

Matthew 6:14–15

If he sins against you seven times in a day, and
seven times comes back to you and says, 'I
repent,' forgive him."

Luke 17:4

FEBRUARY 1

One encouraging word
May be all someone needs
To draw them to our Lord
So always plant those seeds

In that word they will see
That they are truly loved
And worthy to receive
Grace and mercy from our Beloved

An anxious heart weighs a man down, but a kind word cheers him up.

Proverbs 12:25

Finally, all of you, live in harmony with one another; be sympathetic, love as brothers, be compassionate and humble.

1 Peter 3:8

And we urge you, brothers, warn those who are idle, encourage the timid, help the weak, be patient with everyone.

1 Thessalonians 5:14

FEBRUARY 2

Today I lift You up
I offer You my praise
For every day I see
The beauty in Your ways

So I sing in joy
In You I do rejoice
You fill my heart so full
To share I have no choice

Let the name of the Lord be praised, both now and forevermore. From the rising of the sun to the place where it sets, the name of the Lord is to be praised.

Psalm 113:2–3

Great is the Lord and most worthy of praise; his greatness no one can fathom.

Psalm 145:3

Shout for joy to the Lord, all the earth. Worship the Lord with gladness; come before him with joyful songs.

Psalm 100:1–2

FEBRUARY 3

You know when you're in a slump
And you don't know what to do
If you turn to Jesus
He will pull you through

Focus on Him
All throughout your day
The fulfillment that brings
Will chase your blues away

Comfort, comfort my people, says your God.
Isaiah 40:1

Finally, brothers, whatever is true, whatever is noble, whatever is right, whatever is pure, whatever is lovely, whatever is admirable—if anything is excellent or praiseworthy—think about such things.
Philippians 4:8

He said to them, "Why are you troubled, and why do doubts rise in your minds?
Luke 24:38

FEBRUARY 4

There are just days
You don't want to get out of bed
However, if you have purpose
You want to spring ahead

So put your faith in God
Seek His plan for you
This will give you joy
And direction in all you do

If the Lord delights in a man's way, he makes his steps firm; though he stumble, he will not fall, for the Lord upholds him with his hand.
Psalm 37:23–24

always giving thanks to God the Father for everything, in the name of our Lord Jesus Christ.
Ephesians 5:20

So with you: Now is your time of grief, but I will see you again and you will rejoice, and no one will take away your joy.
John 16:22

FEBRUARY 5

I am surrounded by His beauty
Every which way I turn
To see a miracle
I no longer yearn

For once I opened my heart
To Jesus Christ our Lord
I am amazed daily
In His action and His word

Delight yourself in the Lord and he will give you
the desires of your heart.

Psalm 37:4

Jesus replied, "What is impossible with men is
possible with God."

Luke 18:27

He performs wonders that cannot be fathomed,
miracles that cannot be counted.

Job 5:9

FEBRUARY 6

Like the wings of a butterfly
So intricate and true
Are the promises of Jesus
For me and for you

He will never leave us
And fills us with His love
His joy in many colors
A blessed gift from above

In his hand is the life of every creature and the breath of all mankind.

Job 12:10

the Lord make his face shine upon you and be gracious to you;

Numbers 6:25

Though the mountains be shaken and the hills be removed, yet my unfailing love for you will not be shaken nor my covenant of peace be removed," says the Lord, who has compassion on you.

Isaiah 54:10

FEBRUARY 7

Today I start a new day
To seek and learn and grow
I turn my eyes toward Jesus
And in my heart I know

I am not alone
He guides every step I take
He will always love me
With every move I make

I love those who love me, and those who seek me find me.

Proverbs 8:17

"'If you can'?" said Jesus. "Everything is possible for him who believes."

Mark 9:23

Therefore we do not lose heart. Though outwardly we are wasting away, yet inwardly we are being renewed day by day.

2 Corinthians 4:16

FEBRUARY 8

If I were a tree
Of the Holy Spirit
What fruits would I bear
And would others see it

If they saw it upon my face
Or heard it in my voice
Would they want that too
If given the choice

But the fruit of the Spirit is love, joy, peace, patience, kindness, goodness, faithfulness,
Galatians 5:22

We know that we live in him and he in us, because he has given us of his Spirit. And we have seen and testify that the Father has sent his Son to be the Savior of the world.
1 John 4:13–14

"Therefore I tell you that the kingdom of God will be taken away from you and given to a people who will produce its fruit.
Matthew 21:43

FEBRUARY 9

What will be my big thing today
That I may face or go through
I know I will see it differently
If I just magnify You

Nothing will be too big
And I will feel six feet tall
If I remember to trust You
And focus on You through it all

Is any one of you in trouble? He should pray. Is
anyone happy? Let him sing songs of praise.
James 5:13

The righteous cry out, and the Lord hears them;
he delivers them from all their troubles.
Psalm 34:17

You will keep in perfect peace him whose mind is
steadfast, because he trusts in you.
Isaiah 26:3

FEBRUARY 10

We pray for what we want
But that's the wrong thing to do
We need to pray for God's will
In the lives of me and you

We should praise Him
Give thanks for what He has done
Lift up those you love
Trust the timing of our Holy One

But as for me, I watch in hope for the Lord, I wait for God my Savior; my God will hear me.
Micah 7:7

But do not forget this one thing, dear friends: With the Lord a day is like a thousand years, and a thousand years are like a day. The Lord is not slow in keeping his promise, as some understand slowness. He is patient with you, not wanting anyone to perish, but everyone to come to repentance.
2 Peter 3:8–9

When you ask, you do not receive, because you ask with wrong motives, that you may spend what you get on your pleasures.
James 4:3

FEBRUARY 11

Lord help me remember
There will be those in life
That seem to want to harm
And bring others strife

My goal is not to stop them
I can't control what they do
I am to live like Jesus
And leave their conviction to You

keeping a clear conscience, so that those who speak maliciously against your good behavior in Christ may be ashamed of their slander.
1 Peter 3:16

"If the world hates you, keep in mind that it hated me first.
John 15:18

When justice is done, it brings joy to the righteous but terror to evildoers.
Proverbs 21:15

FEBRUARY 12

In You let me show joy
Let me be excited in Your word
For it brings eternal life
The most beautiful thing I've ever heard

There is no greater gift
Not even silver and gold
Are more precious than
The good news I've been told

And how can they preach unless they are sent? As it is written, "How beautiful are the feet of those who bring good news!"
Romans 10:15

My fruit is better than fine gold; what I yield surpasses choice silver.
Proverbs 8:19

Sing to him, sing praise to him; tell of all his wonderful acts. Glory in his holy name; let the hearts of those who seek the Lord rejoice.
Psalm 105:2–3

FEBRUARY 13

God even puts beauty in the thorns
If we look close enough
Try to see what is inside
And find it's not that tuff

Take a beautiful purple thistle
Will poke you if given a chance
Yet gracefully sustains life
It is more than its circumstance

Your beauty should not come from outward adornment, such as braided hair and the wearing of gold jewelry and fine clothes. Instead, it should be that of your inner self, the unfading beauty of a gentle and quiet spirit, which is of great worth in God's sight.
1 Peter 3:3–4

Through him all things were made; without him nothing was made that has been made.
John 1:3

In his hand are the depths of the earth, and the mountain peaks belong to him.
Psalm 95:4

FEBRUARY 14

We were not promised
Happiness every day of our life
But an inner joy
To carry us through any strife

For we will have troubles
And we will get sad
But our Savior will always be there
For that I am glad

Consider it pure joy, my brothers, whenever you face trials of many kinds, because you know that the testing of your faith develops perseverance.
James 1:2–3

I pray that out of his glorious riches he may strengthen you with power through his Spirit in your inner being,
Ephesians 3:16

So with you: Now is your time of grief, but I will see you again and you will rejoice, and no one will take away your joy.
John 16:22

FEBRUARY 15

Open my eyes to see
The world as You do
Fill me with vision
And make my heart true

True to hear Your yearnings
To feel compassion and love
True to Your path for me
With divine guidance from above

By this all men will know that you are my disci-
ples, if you love one another."
John 13:35

Ears that hear and eyes that see—the Lord has
made them both.
Proverbs 20:12

Your attitude should be the same as that of Christ
Jesus:
Philippians 2:5

FEBRUARY 16

Draw me close to You
And what I need to hear
From Your unchanging word
For this day, this month, this year

May I take the time
To remember You and pray
And listen to Your guidance
For this year, this month, this day

Every good and perfect gift is from above, coming down from the Father of the heavenly lights, who does not change like shifting shadows.
James 1:17

But the plans of the Lord stand firm forever, the purposes of his heart through all generations.
Psalm 33:11

The grass withers and the flowers fall, but the word of our God stands forever."
Isaiah 40:8

FEBRUARY 17

Your coat of many colors
Is wrapped around this earth
If we could only take it
For exactly what it is worth

It is Your peace
Your love and Your grace
Together they fill my heart with joy
And shine upon my face

All the earth bows down to you; they sing praise
to you, they sing praise to your name."
Psalm 66:4

For as high as the heavens are above the earth, so
great is his love for those who fear him;
Psalm 103:11

but accepts men from every nation who fear him
and do what is right.
Acts 10:35

FEBRUARY 18

Today is the day
I stand up to my fears
You will rob me no more
As I shed joyful tears

For I am worthy
And I am loved
I am a gift from God
Sent down from above

The Lord is compassionate and gracious, slow to anger, abounding in love.

Psalm 103:8

For I am the Lord, your God, who takes hold of your right hand and says to you, Do not fear; I will help you.

Isaiah 41:13

I sought the Lord, and he answered me; he delivered me from all my fears.

Psalm 34:4

FEBRUARY 19

Today I will listen
To the little voice in my head
By saying that special word or prayer
For someone when I'm led

I may never know
What my sentiment will mean
Yet I will have peace
If on the holy spirit I lean

Do not withhold good from those who deserve it, when it is in your power to act.
Proverbs 3:27

Therefore encourage one another and build each other up, just as in fact you are doing.
1 Thessalonians 5:11

Pleasant words are a honeycomb, sweet to the soul and healing to the bones.
Proverbs 16:24

FEBRUARY 20

Part of my being happy
Is knowing what to do
When I see and hear things
That are wonderful for you

I shall not be jealous
Or turn green with envy
I will be happy for you
And aware of the blessings in me

And I saw that all labor and all achievement spring from man's envy of his neighbor. This too is meaningless, a chasing after the wind.
Ecclesiastes 4:4

A heart at peace gives life to the body, but envy rots the bones.
Proverbs 14:30

Our mouths were filled with laughter, our tongues with songs of joy. Then it was said among the nations, "The Lord has done great things for them."
Psalm 126:2

FEBRUARY 21

Each day isn't perfect
Of that I am aware
It doesn't mean I am not loved
And no one out there cares

For when I am weak
My Lord is strong
And He cares for me
All the day long

We are glad whenever we are weak but you are strong; and our prayer is for your perfection.
2 Corinthians 13:9

It is God who arms me with strength and makes my way perfect.
Psalm 18:32

That is why, for Christ's sake, I delight in weaknesses, in insults, in hardships, in persecutions, in difficulties. For when I am weak, then I am strong.
2 Corinthians 12:10

Don't be discouraged
When you see me cry
It doesn't mean I lack trust
In our Lord up high

For I am human
And emotions may abound
Yet I still know Jesus
That's where my true joy is found

He will wipe every tear from their eyes. There will be no more death or mourning or crying or pain, for the old order of things has passed away."
Revelation 21:4

Record my lament; list my tears on your scroll—are they not in your record?
Psalm 56:8

Jesus wept.

John 11:35

FEBRUARY 23

What can I do
To be closer to God
How do I find balance
Without feeling flawed

You only have time
For what you make time for
So my extra moments
I'll be seeking Him evermore

I will extol the Lord at all times; his praise will
always be on my lips.
Psalm 34:1

Teach us to number our days aright, that we may
gain a heart of wisdom.
Psalm 90:12

Trust in him at all times, O people; pour out
your hearts to him, for God is our refuge.
Psalm 62:8

FEBRUARY 24

As I look in the mirror
What do I really see
Who is the person
Looking back at me

It is someone I love
Because I am a child of God
My heart is full of Him
So I just smile and nod

Yet to all who received him, to those who believed in his name, he gave the right to become children of God—

John 1:12

He who gets wisdom loves his own soul; he who cherishes understanding prospers.

Proverbs 19:8

How great is the love the Father has lavished on us, that we should be called children of God! And that is what we are! The reason the world does not know us is that it did not know him.

1 John 3:1

FEBRUARY 25

So many struggle
With life's ups and downs
Wondering where to turn
Why so many frowns

There is one true way
To find your inner joy
Let Jesus in your heart
That sadness He will destroy

for, "Everyone who calls on the name of the Lord
will be saved."
Romans 10:13

Taste and see that the Lord is good; blessed is the
man who takes refuge in him.
Psalm 34:8

He heals the brokenhearted and binds up their
wounds.
Psalm 147:3

FEBRUARY 26

*You say you don't
Have to make a choice
I'm saying you do
No opinion is still your voice*

*For if you choose yes
Or if you choose no
Or just not at all
Decides which way you will go*

This day I call heaven and earth as witnesses against you that I have set before you life and death, blessings and curses. Now choose life, so that you and your children may live
Deuteronomy 30:19

But if serving the Lord seems undesirable to you, then choose for yourselves this day whom you will serve, whether the gods your forefathers served beyond the River, or the gods of the Amorites, in whose land you are living. But as for me and my household, we will serve the Lord."
Joshua 24:15

Salvation is found in no one else, for there is no other name under heaven given to men by which we must be saved."

Acts 4:12

FEBRUARY 27

We are shown
Time and time again
Life is too short
So now is the time to begin

Put down your tasks
Take time to pray
And ask our Lord above
To guide your steps today

Be very careful, then, how you live—not as unwise but as wise, making the most of every opportunity, because the days are evil. Therefore do not be foolish, but understand what the Lord's will is.
Ephesians 5:15–17

Teach us to number our days aright, that we may gain a heart of wisdom.
Psalm 90:12

I know, O Lord, that a man's life is not his own; it is not for man to direct his steps.
Jeremiah 10:23

FEBRUARY 28

Let us know
There is a season
We are not always full bloom
And for very good reason

There is a time to plant
And a time to grow
So when we do bloom
It is Your love we show

He is like a tree planted by streams of water, which yields its fruit in season and whose leaf does not wither. Whatever he does prospers.
Psalm 1:3

He changes times and seasons; he sets up kings and deposes them. He gives wisdom to the wise and knowledge to the discerning.
Daniel 2:21

I planted the seed, Apollos watered it, but God made it grow.
1 Corinthians 3:6

MARCH 1

How much I give
And what I do
Shows my devotion to Christ
Letting His light shine through

Give with cheer
And where you are led
Not for your own gain
For it's what Christ has said

Each man should give what he has decided in his heart to give, not reluctantly or under compulsion, for God loves a cheerful giver.
2 Corinthians 9:7

For if the willingness is there, the gift is acceptable according to what one has, not according to what he does not have.
2 Corinthians 8:12

In the same way, let your light shine before men, that they may see your good deeds and praise your Father in heaven.
Matthew 5:16

MARCH 2

If you desire peace
You must actively pursue it
Make changes that matter
Let your pride take a hit

Trust God more
Less worry is your goal
You must have faith in Him
And believe He is in control

He must turn from evil and do good; he must seek peace and pursue it.
1 Peter 3:11

Peacemakers who sow in peace raise a harvest of righteousness.
James 3:18

Those who know your name will trust in you, for you, Lord, have never forsaken those who seek you.
Psalm 9:10

I must love me
For I can never get away
It is with myself
I spend every minute of every day

It's a relationship that matters
Though to some seems odd
Without this how do I love others
Or truly love and honor God

Dear friends, let us love one another, for love comes from God. Everyone who loves has been born of God and knows God.
1 John 4:7

Better is a poor man who walks in his integrity than a rich man who is crooked in his ways.
Proverbs 28:6 (ESV)

Restore to me the joy of your salvation and grant me a willing spirit, to sustain me. Then I will teach transgressors your ways, and sinners will turn back to you.
Psalm 51:12–13

MARCH 4

I lift up Your name
For that brings me joy
I know You are here
For each girl and boy

You show us the way
If it's Your will we seek
You give us strength
When we are weak

Clap your hands, all you nations; shout to God with cries of joy.

Psalm 47:1

Your word is a lamp to my feet and a light for my path.

Psalm 119:105

He gives strength to the weary and increases the power of the weak.

Isaiah 40:29

MARCH 5

No matter the failures
I daily do face
My heart is at peace
In Your loving grace

For You are my light
And You show me the way
When I trust in You
The joy in my heart does stay

Let the peace of Christ rule in your hearts, since as members of one body you were called to peace. And be thankful.

Colossians 3:15

And the peace of God, which transcends all understanding, will guard your hearts and your minds in Christ Jesus.

Philippians 4:7

May the God of hope fill you with all joy and peace as you trust in him, so that you may overflow with hope by the power of the Holy Spirit.

Romans 15:13

MARCH 6

When I focus
On the Lord our God
My troubles disappear
Do you find that odd?

Yet I know it's true
He cares for my every need
When my eyes are on Him
My fears do concede

"The eye is the lamp of the body. If your eyes are good, your whole body will be full of light.
Matthew 6:22

You will keep in perfect peace him whose mind is steadfast, because he trusts in you.
Isaiah 26:3

He who trusts in himself is a fool, but he who walks in wisdom is kept safe.
Proverbs 28:26

MARCH 7

I see what I want to see
And hear what I want to hear
Let me choose things that are good
So that it may draw You near

For if I focus
On only the things that are bad
I will miss the blessings
In front of me to be had

Let us choose what is right; let us know among
ourselves what is good.
Job 34:4 (ESV)

Hear this, you foolish and senseless people, who
have eyes but do not see, who have ears but do
not hear:
Jeremiah 5:21

And my God will meet all your needs according
to his glorious riches in Christ Jesus.
Philippians 4:19

MARCH 8

Every day is full
Of ups and downs I face
Regardless of my happenings
The Lord provides me with grace

He turns all things to good
This helps fulfill my purpose
A gift meant for us all
With many more under the surface

And we know that in all things God works for the good of those who love him, who have been called according to his purpose.
Romans 8:28

You intended to harm me, but God intended it for good to accomplish what is now being done, the saving of many lives.
Genesis 50:20

he saved us, not because of righteous things we had done, but because of his mercy.
Titus 3:5

I cannot serve two masters
So daily I must choose
The struggle is all around
And I do not wish to lose

So I put my trust in Him
And ask Him to lead the way
I turn from what is wrong
To follow Him every day

"No servant can serve two masters. Either he will hate the one and love the other, or he will be devoted to the one and despise the other. You cannot serve both God and Money."
Luke 16:13

You cannot drink the cup of the Lord and the cup of demons too; you cannot have a part in both the Lord's table and the table of demons.
1 Corinthians 10:21

Do not be yoked together with unbelievers. For what do righteousness and wickedness have in common? Or what fellowship can light have with darkness?
2 Corinthians 6:14

MARCH 10

I know I am a sinner
Yet I have been set free
For God sent His only son
To die and atone for me

Each day I try my best
With each mistake I humbly repent
Giving thanks for the mercy and grace
He so bountifully has sent

This is love: not that we loved God, but that he loved us and sent his Son as an atoning sacrifice for our sins.

1 John 4:10

But we see Jesus, who was made a little lower than the angels, now crowned with glory and honor because he suffered death, so that by the grace of God he might taste death for everyone.

Hebrews 2:9

if my people, who are called by my name, will humble themselves and pray and seek my face and turn from their wicked ways, then will I hear from heaven and will forgive their sin and will heal their land.

2 Chronicles 7:14

MARCH 11

Where will my forever be
Yes this is truly up to me
Do I want my soul to be free
For all of eternity

He gave His life for an enormous fee
So the living waters I could see
If I give my heart to Thee
A beautiful gift, don't you agree

but whoever drinks the water I give him will never thirst. Indeed, the water I give him will become in him a spring of water welling up to eternal life."

John 4:14

Whoever believes in me, as the Scripture has said, streams of living water will flow from within him."

John 7:38

if we endure, we will also reign with him. If we disown him, he will also disown us;

2 Timothy 2:12

MARCH 12

What is it to be thankful
And happy with what you've got
To some it's something so little
Yet others need a lot

Be careful of your yearnings
For no one is better than the other
Don't take more than you need
And be mindful of your brother

Then he said to them, "Watch out! Be on your guard against all kinds of greed; a man's life does not consist in the abundance of his possessions."
Luke 12:15

Do nothing out of selfish ambition or vain conceit, but in humility consider others better than yourselves. Each of you should look not only to your own interests, but also to the interest of others.
Philippians 2:3–4

If anyone has material possessions and sees his brother in need but has no pity on him, how can the love of God be in him?
1 John 3:17

MARCH 13

Forgiveness is such a big word
It's actions seldom seen
Yet it is often heard
What does it truly mean

We speak of it as if
Just saying it is enough
Yet it must fill our hearts
And be shared no matter how tough

Forgive us our debts, as we also have forgiven our debtors.

Matthew 6:12

And when you stand praying, if you hold anything against anyone, forgive him, so that your Father in heaven may forgive you your sins."

Mark 11:25

Therefore, as God's chosen people, holy and dearly loved, clothe yourselves with compassion, kindness, humility, gentleness and patience. Bear with each other and forgive whatever grievances you may have against one another. Forgive as the Lord forgave you.

Colossians 3:12–13

MARCH 14

We get up each morning
And prepare ourselves for the day
Tell me why we don't make time
For our spiritual life and pray

Shouldn't eternity be more important
Than the world outside our door
So take a moment with Jesus
Before your feet hit the floor

Devote yourselves to prayer, being watchful and thankful.

Colossians 4:2

Very early in the morning, while it was still dark, Jesus got up, left the house and went off to a solitary place, where he prayed.

Mark 1:35

Let the morning bring me word of your unfailing love, for I have put my trust in you. Show me the way I should go, for to you I lift up my soul.

Psalm 143:8

MARCH 15

Sometimes my past mistakes
Creep into my mind
Taking my precious today
Why can't they stay behind

I must remember God's promise
That He has made me new
And my past is gone to Him
I need to make it gone too

Therefore, if anyone is in Christ, he is a new creation; the old has gone, the new has come!
2 Corinthians 5:17

"I, even I, am he who blots out your transgressions, for my own sake, and remembers your sins no more.
Isaiah 43:25

Therefore, since we are surrounded by so great a cloud of witnesses, let us also lay aside every weight, and sin which clings so closely, and let us run with endurance the race that is set before us,
Hebrews 12:1 (ESV)

MARCH 16

Let me rejoice
In His holy name!
For if I turn to Him
Nothing will be the same

I will be set free
From my sin and shame
My heart filled with joy
Praising the day He came

Then will I ever sing praise to your name and
fulfill my vows day after day.

Psalm 61:8

Rejoice in the Lord always. I will say it again:
Rejoice!

Philippians 4:4

Shouts of joy and victory resound in the tents of
the righteous: "The Lord's right hand has done
mighty things!

Psalm 118:15

MARCH 17

If someone is special to you
Be sure to let them know
We are not promised tomorrow
Or given the time we will go

Don't miss the opportunity
To share all your love
It is a gift made to give
From our Father up above

Why, you do not even know what will happen tomorrow. What is your life? You are a mist that appears for a little while and then vanishes.
James 4:14

Teach us to number our days aright, that we may gain a heart of wisdom.
Psalm 90:12

The goal of this command is love, which comes from a pure heart and a good conscience and a sincere faith.
1 Timothy 1:5

MARCH 18

Seeking someone's approval
Can be a consuming treacherous act
Yet the approval we seek should be
Our Heavenly Fathers to be exact

For He is our final judgement
And it is His will we should follow
Trying to please the world
Will leave you empty and hollow

Am I now trying to win the approval of men, or of God? Or am I trying to please men? If I were still trying to please men, I would not be a servant of Christ.

Galatians 1:10

Fear of man will prove to be a snare, but whoever trusts in the Lord is kept safe.

Proverbs 29:25

On the contrary, we speak as men approved by God to be entrusted with the gospel. We are not trying to please men but God, who tests our hearts.

1 Thessalonians 2:4

When I walk
With our Lord every day
It eases my mind
And chases the gloom away

I still face trials
Things happen beyond my control
Putting all my trust in Him
Is the ultimate goal

"I have told you these things, so that in me you may have peace. In this world you will have trouble. But take heart! I have overcome the world."
John 16:33

When anxiety was great within me, your consolation brought joy to my soul.
Psalm 94:19

The Lord is my strength and my shield; my heart trusts in him, and I am helped. My heart leaps for joy and I will give thanks to him in song.
Psalm 28:7

MARCH 20

Day in and day out
I am doing the same thing
My mind begins to wonder
What kind of glory this brings

I must always remember
No matter how big or small
If I'm doing in the name of Jesus
I give Him the glory for it all

Whatever you do, work at it with all your heart,
as working for the Lord, not for men,
Colossians 3:23

So whether you eat or drink or whatever you do,
do it all for the glory of God.
1 Corinthians 10:31

Commit to the Lord whatever you do, and your
plans will succeed.
Proverbs 16:3

MARCH 21

As I rise up each morning
And wonder what there is to do
I remember to stop and pray
And give my day to You

For if I listen
To Your will for my day
It goes so much smoother
And I feel better along the way

They are new every morning; great is your faithfulness.

Lamentations 3:23

But seek first his kingdom and his righteousness, and all these things will be given to you as well.

Matthew 6:33

Many are the plans in a man's heart, but it is the Lord's purpose that prevails.

Proverbs 19:21

MARCH 22

This life is so wonderous
If we let it be
God does things for our good
When we open our hearts and see

He is for us every step
Right beside us all the way
Just learn to walk in His timing
Every minute of every day

He has made everything beautiful in its time. He has also set eternity in the hearts of men; yet they cannot fathom what God has done from beginning to end.

Ecclesiastes 3:11

But do not forget this one thing, dear friends: With the Lord a day is like a thousand years, and a thousand years are like a day.

2 Peter 3:8

You intended to harm me, but God intended it for good to accomplish what is now being done, the saving of many lives.

Genesis 50:20

MARCH 23

I know better
Yet here I sit
I let the devil
Win this bet

For in this round
I did choose wrong
The games not over
He won't win for long

I do not understand what I do. For what I want to do I do not do, but what I hate I do.
Romans 7:15

No temptation has seized you except what is common to man. And God is faithful; he will not let you be tempted beyond what you can bear. But when you are tempted, he will also provide a way out so that you can stand up under it.
1 Corinthians 10:13

Many are the plans in a man's heart, but it is the Lord's purpose that prevails.
Proverbs 19:21

When I feel useless
Or I'm feeling unloved
I need to look up
To our Lord above

For He is the measure
Of my true worth
And loves me more
Than all the earth

Indeed, the very hairs of your head are all numbered. Don't be afraid; you are worth more than many sparrows.

Luke 12:7

I praise you because I am fearfully and wonderfully made; your works are wonderful, I know that full well.

Psalm 139:14

The Lord your God is with you, he is mighty to save. He will take great delight in you, he will quiet you with his love, he will rejoice over you with singing."

Zephaniah 3:17

MARCH 25

Have you ever been bit by a mosquito
Well yes, I reply
Have you ever been bit by an elephant
No, I respond, wondering as to why

It's the little things
That will get you every time
So rise above the small stuff
And you will feel sublime

Do not be anxious about anything, but in every-
thing, by prayer and petition, with thanksgiving,
present your requests to God.
Philippians 4:6

"Do not let your hearts be troubled. Trust in
God; trust also in me.
John 14:1

Who of you by worrying can add a single hour
to his life?
Matthew 6:27

MARCH 26

Some days are just hard
To know what to do
Then I must refocus
And turn my eyes to You

You give me strength
And never leave me behind
Always in You
A comfort I do find

The Lord himself goes before you and will be
with you; he will never leave you nor forsake you.
Do not be afraid; do not be discouraged."
Deuteronomy 31:8

Cast your cares on the Lord and he will sustain
you; he will never let the righteous fall.
Psalm 55:22

May the Lord our God be with us as he was with
our fathers; may he never leave us nor forsake us.
1 Kings 8:57

MARCH 27

Today my heart is heavy
An emotion I can feel
How do I lighten the pain
And begin to heal

I must focus on You
And the promises You made
By surrendering thoughts to You
My burden begins to fade

Cast all your anxiety on him because he cares for you.

1 Peter 5:7

Peace I leave with you; my peace I give you. I do not give to you as the world gives. Do not let your hearts be troubled and do not be afraid.

John 14:27

"Yet if you devote your heart to him and stretch out your hands to him,

Job 11:13

MARCH 28

Situations are many
That I don't know what to say
My mind will run in circles
Not finding its way

Then I must take a moment
And ask You to speak through me
For the Holy Spirit guides us
If we calm down and let it be

Then the Lord reached out his hand and touched my mouth and said to me, "Now, I have put my words in your mouth.
                    Jeremiah 1:9

for the Holy Spirit will teach you at that time what you should say."
                    Luke 12:12

for it will not be you speaking, but the Spirit of your Father speaking through you.
                    Matthew 10:20

MARCH 29

There is no burden too big
That with You I cannot face
If I have faith and believe
Securely in Your grace

I give it all to you Lord
The one I truly trust
For I know You are with me
Always loving and just

"I am the Lord, the God of all mankind. Is anything too hard for me?
                    Jeremiah 32:27

Trust in him at all times, O people; pour out your hearts to him, for God is our refuge.
                    Psalm 62:8

And without faith it is impossible to please God, because anyone who comes to him must believe that he exists and that he rewards those who earnestly seek him.
                    Hebrews 11:6

MARCH 30

I sit and listen
To the birds sing
As the leaves rustle in the wind
It makes me think of one thing

What a beautiful world
Our Lord has created
Praising and thanking Him
Makes me feel elated

How many are your works, O Lord! In wisdom you made them all; the earth is full of your creatures.

Psalm 104:24

The heavens declare the glory of God; the skies proclaim the work of his hands.

Psalm 19:1

And God said, "Let the water teem with living creatures, and let birds fly above the earth across the expanse of the sky."

Genesis 1:20

MARCH 31

I don't like roller coasters
And avoid them at all cost
Yet sometimes things beyond my control
Make me feel that effort is lost

For my life may be steady
While my loved ones are not
Through their ups and downs I go
On their ride I am caught

Therefore encourage one another and build each
other up, just as in fact you are doing.
1 Thessalonians 5:11

And let us consider how we may spur one another
on toward love and good deeds.
Hebrews 10:24

If one member suffers, all suffer together; if one
member is honored, all rejoice together.
1 Corinthians 12:26 (ESV)

APRIL 1

Love one another
For this is His command
Be it enemy or friend
Pray and make your stand

Forgive each other
Be proud and make it known
In this God made us able
So that no-one feels alone

But I tell you: Love your enemies and pray for those who persecute you,
> Matthew 5:44

My command is this: Love each other as I have loved you.
> John 15:12

Forgive us our debts, as we also have forgiven our debtors.
> Matthew 6:12

APRIL 2

Each day is precious
For tomorrow may not come
Don't let others wonder
Where your joy is from

Be sure to share the good news
Of our Savior's love
And how wonderful it will be
To spend eternity in heaven above

I pray that you may be active in sharing your faith, so that you will have a full understanding of every good thing we have in Christ.

Philemon 1:6

But in your hearts set apart Christ as Lord. Always be prepared to give an answer to everyone who asks you to give the reason for the hope that you have. But do this with gentleness and respect,

1 Peter 3:15

Sing to the Lord, praise his name; proclaim his salvation day after day.

Psalm 96:2

APRIL 3

There are so many things
That throw our life off track
How do we start over
And get our sanity back

One sure way I know
God will straighten me out
With patience and love
I have no doubt

in all your ways acknowledge him, and he will
make your paths straight.
Proverbs 3:6

and call upon me in the day of trouble; I will
deliver you, and you will honor me."
Psalm 50:15

If we confess our sins, he is faithful and just and
will forgive us our sins and purify us from all
unrighteousness.
1 John 1:9

APRIL 4

Struggles are not biased
Rich, poor, young and old
They plague us all
So I have been told

Although they are all different
The answer is the same
No matter who or where you are
Just call on His precious name

Because he turned his ear to me, I will call on him as long as I live.
Psalm 116:2

And the God of all grace, who called you to his eternal glory in Christ, after you have suffered a little while, will himself restore you and make you strong, firm and steadfast.
1 Peter 5:10

When the Pharisees saw this, they asked his disciples, "Why does your teacher eat with tax collectors and 'sinners'?"
Matthew 9:11

APRIL 5

Sometimes we lose things
That really mean a lot
And when it's someone we love
We may feel our life is all for naught

But we all have our own purpose
We are worthy to make it through
Move beyond this moment
And embrace the new you

The Lord is close to the brokenhearted and saves
those who are crushed in spirit.
Psalm 34:18

Blessed are those who mourn, for they will be
comforted.
Matthew 5:4

Do not conform any longer to the pattern of
this world, but be transformed by the renewing
of your mind. Then you will be able to test and
approve what God's will is—his good, pleasing
and perfect will.
Romans 12:2

APRIL 6

Oh ye of little faith
Hand your troubles over to God
Believe He will handle them
Don't stay where others trod

It may not be what you want
Or when you want it to be
But it will be for your good
Just be patient, you will see

"Do not let your hearts be troubled. Trust in God; trust also in me.
John 14:1

Perseverance must finish its work so that you may be mature and complete, not lacking anything.
James 1:4

Wait for the Lord; be strong and take heart and wait for the Lord.
Psalm 27:14

APRIL 7

Plant a seed
When you get a chance
You may not see it grow
Yet it must be started to advance

Let the body of Christ
Help you cultivate and harvest
And the Holy Spirit will come forward
When He knows it is best

The man who plants and the man who waters have one purpose, and each will be rewarded according to his own labor.
1 Corinthians 3:8

"This is the meaning of the parable: The seed is the word of God.
Luke 8:11

Let us not become weary in doing good, for at the proper time we will reap a harvest if we do not give up.
Galatians 6:9

APRIL 8

Gifts are a funny thing
Are they to be given or to receive
Or can it be both in one
This is true when you believe

For we each are given a gift
That is to be shared as we serve
And we are blessing while being blessed
Far beyond what we deserve

Each one should use whatever gift he has received to serve others, faithfully administering God's grace in its various forms.

1 Peter 4:10

Whoever brings blessings will be enriched, and one who waters will himself be watered.

Proverbs 11:25 (ESV)

In everything I did, I showed you that by this kind of hard work we must help the weak, remembering the words the Lord Jesus himself said: 'It is more blessed to give than to receive.'"

Acts 20:35

APRIL 9

How do I lift my spirits
I sing praises to Your name
And seek the Holy Spirit
Then I don't feel the same

My heart it is lighter
There is a sweetness in my voice
Getting here to this moment
Is a conscious choice

And whatever you do, whether in word or deed, do it all in the name of the Lord Jesus, giving thanks to God the Father through him.
Colossians 3:17

Praise the Lord, O my soul; all my inmost being, praise his holy name.
Psalm 103:1

So what shall I do? I will pray with my spirit, but I will also pray with my mind; I will sing with my spirit, but I will also sing with my mind.
1 Corinthians 14:15

APRIL 10

Our Lord is contagious
He brings us such joy
The deeper you get in His word
A desire for Him does deploy

For the more I learn
The more I want to know
By praying, sharing and study
What a wonderful way to grow

But his delight is in the law of the Lord, and on his law he meditates day and night.
Psalm 1:2

When your words came, I ate them; they were my joy and my heart's delight, for I bear your name, O Lord God Almighty.
Jeremiah 15:16

But grow in the grace and knowledge of our Lord and Savior Jesus Christ. To him be glory both now and forever! Amen.
2 Peter 3:18

APRIL 11

We are told to pray
And listen to God's will
That He tells us what to do
If we will only be still

Realize the answer
May not be a flashing sign
But just a gentle peace and comfort
Knowing your direction is fine

I have considered my ways and have turned my steps to your statutes.

Psalm 119:59

For God does speak—now one way, now another—though man may not perceive it.

Job 33:14

Do not conform any longer to the pattern of this world, but be transformed by the renewing of your mind. Then you will be able to test and approve what God's will is—his good, pleasing and perfect will.

Romans 12:2

APRIL 12

Always be thankful
For what you've got
It's all a gift from God
And it should mean a lot

Whatever your complaining about
Someone out there is praying for
So change your outlook
To be grateful forever more

give thanks in all circumstances, for this is God's will for you in Christ Jesus.
1 Thessalonians 5:18

Thanks be to God for his indescribable gift!
2 Corinthians 9:15

I know what it is to be in need, and I know what it is to have plenty. I have learned the secret of being content in any and every situation, whether well fed or hungry, whether living in plenty or in want.
Philippians 4:12

APRIL 13

Silence is golden
Not only to set in
And enjoy the moment
But in knowing where to begin

It gives you time to think
Pray, weigh and measure
And to give a response
That brings peace and pleasure

My dear brothers, take note of this: Everyone should be quick to listen, slow to speak and slow to become angry,

James 1:19

Even a fool is thought wise if he keeps silent, and discerning if he holds his tongue.

Proverbs 17:28

May the words of my mouth and the meditation of my heart be pleasing in your sight, O Lord, my Rock and my Redeemer.

Psalm 19:14

APRIL 14

Family is something different
To everyone we meet
For some it's only kin
And others anyone on the street

We are all brothers and sisters
In the eyes of God
And He is our Father
We should be like peas in a pod

so in Christ we who are many form one body,
and each member belongs to all the others.
Romans 12:5

"I will be a Father to you, and you will be my
sons and daughters, says the Lord Almighty."
2 Corinthians 6:18

There is neither Jew nor Greek, slave nor free,
male nor female, for you are all one in Christ
Jesus.
Galatians 3:28

APRIL 15

I read from my bible
And trust in His word
Yet why do I not apply
All that I have heard

It seems so simple
Although extremely hard
To humble myself daily
And let down my guard

Then Jesus said to his disciples, "If anyone would come after me, he must deny himself and take up his cross and follow me.
Matthew 16:24

I seek you with all my heart; do not let me stray from your commands.
Psalm 119:10

Do your best to present yourself to God as one approved, a workman who does not need to be ashamed and who correctly handles the word of truth.
2 Timothy 2:15

APRIL 16

When your life is overwhelming
And you really don't know why
There is something that brings peace
If you sincerely try

Turn your worries over to God
For He truly does care for you
Always loving and understanding
Together there is nothing you can't do

Jesus looked at them and said, "With man this is impossible, but with God all things are possible."
Matthew 19:26

In God, whose word I praise, in God I trust; I will not be afraid. What can mortal man do to me?

Psalm 56:4

You will surely forget your trouble, recalling it only as waters gone by.
Job 11:16

APRIL 17

Success is important
But at what cost
Be careful how you get it
Don't act like the lost

You can reach your goals
With your integrity intact
Just climb the ladder with Jesus
And be mindful of how you act

Commit to the Lord whatever you do, and your plans will succeed.

Proverbs 16:3

and observe what the Lord your God requires: Walk in his ways, and keep his decrees and commands, his laws and requirements, as written in the Law of Moses, so that you may prosper in all you do and wherever you go,

1 Kings 2:3

What good will it be for a man if he gains the whole world, yet forfeits his soul? Or what can a man give in exchange for his soul?

Matthew 16:26

Prayer is a powerful thing
Communication with God is key
Yes He knows our every need
Yet still loves talking with you and me

We must lift up those that are lost
And pray for physical needs
Give thanks for all He has done
And for the courage to plant His seeds

Devote yourselves to prayer, being watchful and thankful.

Colossians 4:2

Then you will call upon me and come and pray to me, and I will listen to you.

Jeremiah 29:12

And pray in the Spirit on all occasions with all kinds of prayers and requests.

Ephesians 6:18

APRIL 19

People will try to break you
Whether they realize it or not
You have a choice to make
Either get them or be got

Stand strong in your faith
Be humble, loving and kind
Do not return the favor
And it will blow their mind

Do not repay anyone evil for evil. Be careful to do what is right in the eyes of everybody.
Romans 12:17

When they hurled their insults at him, he did not retaliate; when he suffered, he made no threats. Instead, he entrusted himself to him who judges justly.
1 Peter 2:23

Do not repay evil with evil or insult with insult, but with blessing, because to this you were called so that you may inherit a blessing.
1 Peter 3:9

APRIL 20

What a blessing it is
To share God's word
It lifts up the speaker
And everyone that has heard

For there aren't enough people
That are willing to share
And if we don't tell others
It just doesn't seem fair

Declare his glory among the nations, his marvelous deeds among all peoples.
Psalm 96:3

He said to them, "Go into all the world and preach the good news to all creation.
Mark 16:15

I pray that you may be active in sharing your faith, so that you will have a full understanding of every good thing we have in Christ.
Philemon 1:6

APRIL 21

Distractions are everywhere
Designed to take us away
From God's perfect love
Each and every day

So we must be disciplined
And not give in
Committing to study and prayer
Turning away from sin

At one time we too were foolish, disobedient, deceived and enslaved by all kinds of passions and pleasures. We lived in malice and envy, being hated and hating one another.

Titus 3:3

Turn my eyes away from worthless things; preserve my life according to your word.

Psalm 119:37

So I say, live by the Spirit, and you will not gratify the desires of the sinful nature.

Galatians 5:16

APRIL 22

Watch what you do
Because you don't know who is watching
You don't want to ruin your witness
Or your actions to be botching

You want your actions to be fruitful
And lift up His holy name
To draw others closer
Wanting them to seek the same

Keep watch over yourselves and all the flock of which the Holy Spirit has made you overseers.
Acts 20:28

Be wise in the way you act toward outsiders; make the most of every opportunity.
Colossians 4:5

You, my brothers, were called to be free. But do not use your freedom to indulge the sinful nature; rather, serve one another in love.
Galatians 5:13

APRIL 23

How many daily blessings
Do we take for granted
Not being thankful
For the time and place we are planted

We have cars and homes
And food on our table
Can worship our God freely
Or do about anything we are able

Therefore, since we are receiving a kingdom that cannot be shaken, let us be thankful, and so worship God acceptably with reverence and awe,
Hebrews 12:28

But if we have food and clothing, we will be content with that.
1 Timothy 6:8

I am not saying this because I am in need, for I have learned to be content whatever the circumstances.
Philippians 4:11

APRIL 24

Why is it so hard
For us to have faith and believe
Even the ones long ago
Watching miracles couldn't perceive

If we think one part is true
Shouldn't we trust it all
Everything doesn't always make sense
Have you answered your call

Now faith is being sure of what we hope for and
certain of what we do not see.
Hebrews 11:1

By faith the people passed through the Red Sea as
on dry land; but when the Egyptians tried to do
so, they were drowned.
Hebrews 11:29

The Lord said to Moses, "How long will these
people treat me with contempt? How long will
they refuse to believe in me, in spite of all the
miraculous signs I have performed among them?
Numbers 14:11

APRIL 25

Do you ever take a moment
To look around and actually see
The beauty that surrounds you
That was made for you and me

All the greens in the forest
Every flower you pass by
The wind that blows your hair
And all the colors in the sky

Thus the heavens and the earth were completed in all their vast array.
Genesis 2:1

In his hand is the life of every creature and the breath of all mankind.
Job 12:10

Do you know how the clouds hang poised, those wonders of him who is perfect in knowledge?
Job 37:16

APRIL 26

Before I met Jesus
I thought I was content
Yet I saw the joy in others
And didn't know what it meant

Then He called my name
And pulled at my heart strings
I gave my life to Him
Giving new meaning to all things

You have made known to me the path of life; you will fill me with joy in your presence, with eternal pleasures at your right hand.

Psalm 16:11

for God's gifts and his call are irrevocable.

Romans 11:29

For you were once darkness, but now you are light in the Lord. Live as children of light (for the fruit of the light consists in all goodness, righteousness and truth)

Ephesians 5:8–9

APRIL 27

Our Lord is wonderful
He fills my cup
I can't imagine life
If I gave this all up

He gives me comfort
When I'm feeling down
He brings me joy
He is my solid ground

May all who seek you rejoice and be glad in you!
May those who love your salvation say evermore,
"God is great!"

Psalm 70:4 (ESV)

With joy you will draw water from the wells of
salvation.

Isaiah 12:3

He said: "The Lord is my rock, my fortress and
my deliverer; my God is my rock, in whom I take
refuge, my shield and the horn of my salvation.

2 Samuel 22:2–3

APRIL 28

I don't say thank you enough
To those who matter most
And I'm not talking about
The Father, Son and Holy Ghost

I'm talking about those close
They are to be treated the best
Not as a catch all of negativity
So give your loved ones a rest

Therefore, as we have opportunity, let us do good to all people, especially to those who belong to the family of believers.
Galatians 6:10

Husbands, love your wives and do not be harsh with them.
Colossians 3:19

It is not rude, it is not self-seeking, it is not easily angered, it keeps no record of wrongs.
1 Corinthians 13:5

APRIL 29

As I lay in bed awake
Wondering what the day will bring
It could have been my quiet time
To come to You in prayer on everything

Thanking You for blessing me with another day
Lifting up those in need
Praying Your will be shown to me
And that I will graciously heed

In the morning, O Lord, you hear my voice; in the morning I lay my requests before you and wait in expectation.

Psalm 5:3

O Lord, be gracious to us; we long for you. Be our strength every morning, our salvation in time of distress.

Isaiah 33:2

They are new every morning; great is your faithfulness.

Lamentations 3:23

APRIL 30

My heart is a funny thing
It is softened by Your love
Yet sometimes when I open my mouth
My words aren't soft from above

Sometimes I can't comprehend
The tone and words I say
Please make my mind quiet
And allow my heart to lead the way

If anyone considers himself religious and yet does not keep a tight rein on his tongue, he deceives himself and his religion is worthless.

James 1:26

So in everything, do to others what you would have them do to you, for this sums up the Law and the Prophets.

Matthew 7:12

Set a guard over my mouth, O Lord; keep watch over the door of my lips.

Psalm 141:3

MAY 1

What imprint will we leave
When we go to another life
Will it be of love and grace
Or a path of chaos and strife

Let my actions and words
Leave an imprint of You not me
Help me day to day
Be mindful of what others see

I have been crucified with Christ and I no longer live, but Christ lives in me. The life I live in the body, I live by faith in the Son of God, who loved me and gave himself for me.

Galatians 2:20

When Jesus spoke again to the people, he said, "I am the light of the world. Whoever follows me will never walk in darkness, but will have the light of life."

John 8:12

By this all men will know that you are my disciples, if you love one another."

John 13:35

MAY 2

You figured me out
And reeled me in
Today is the day
My eternity begins

I am so thankful
You never gave up
And You will always
Refill my cup

"No one can come to me unless the Father who sent me draws him, and I will raise him up at the last day.

John 6:44

who has saved us and called us to a holy life—not because of anything we have done but because of his own purpose and grace. This grace was given us in Christ Jesus before the beginning of time,

2 Timothy 1:9

And hope does not disappoint us, because God has poured out his love into our hearts by the Holy Spirit, whom he has given us.

Romans 5:5

MAY 3

The world surrounds us
It can draw you in
Like a sucker punch
Right on the chin

So always be ready
With your escape plan
To do a TKO on the devil
Every chance you can

Again, the devil took him to a very high mountain and showed him all the kingdoms of the world and their splendor.
Matthew 4:8

For if you live according to the sinful nature, you will die; but if by the Spirit you put to death the misdeeds of the body, you will live,
Romans 8:13

Be self-controlled and alert. Your enemy the devil prowls around like a roaring lion looking for someone to devour. Resist him, standing firm in the faith, because you know that your brothers throughout the world are undergoing the same kind of sufferings.
1 Peter 5:8–9

MAY 4

Did you just go through something
And feel like you may not recover
Your heart seems so broken
It seems you will never love another

There is someone with you always
Who can assuredly ease your pain
Mending your heart and mind with care
So you may openly love again

Peace I leave with you; my peace I give you. I
do not give to you as the world gives. Do not let
your hearts be troubled and do not be afraid.

John 14:27

The Lord is close to the brokenhearted and saves
those who are crushed in spirit.

Psalm 34:18

He will wipe every tear from their eyes. There
will be no more death or mourning or crying or
pain, for the old order of things has passed away."

Revelation 21:4

MAY 5

Remember the joy you had
When you first got saved
To learn more about Jesus
Is something you craved

Then we slowed down
And went back to our ways
He is still waiting on you
To climb out of your haze

Though you have not seen him, you love him; and even though you do not see him now, you believe in him and are filled with an inexpressible and glorious joy, for you are receiving the goal of your faith, the salvation of your souls.

1 Peter 1:8–9

Restore to me the joy of your salvation and grant me a willing spirit, to sustain me.

Psalm 51:12

If we confess our sins, he is faithful and just and will forgive us our sins and purify us from all unrighteousness.

1 John 1:9

MAY 6

Don't use God's word
As a way to control
Use it only in love
To save someone's soul

We are to share the good news
And not here to judge
So others want to know more
With a graceful kind nudge

For God did not send his Son into the world to condemn the world, but to save the world through him.

John 3:17

So watch yourselves. "If your brother sins, rebuke him, and if he repents, forgive him. If he sins against you seven times in a day, and seven times comes back to you and says, 'I repent,' forgive him."

Luke 17:3–4

For this is what the Lord has commanded us: "'I have made you a light for the Gentiles, that you may bring salvation to the ends of the earth.'"

Acts 13:47

Don't stop at your start
Or end where you begin
Once you accept Jesus
You must dig in

Get into your bible
Join a group or a class
Pray and come to church
Don't let this opportunity pass

But encourage one another daily, as long as it is called Today, so that none of you may be hardened by sin's deceitfulness.

Hebrews 3:13

As iron sharpens iron, so one man sharpens another.

Proverbs 27:17

so as to walk in a manner worthy of the Lord, fully pleasing to him: bearing fruit in every good work and increasing in the knowledge of God;

Colossians 1:10 (ESV)

MAY 8

Faith is more
Than believing in His name
It's a life experience
With it you will never be the same

Being sure of what we hope for
And certain of what we cannot see
Knowing Jesus is always here
Is the faith I want for me

Now faith is being sure of what we hope for and
certain of what we do not see.
Hebrews 11:1

Be strong and courageous. Do not be afraid or
terrified because of them, for the Lord your God
goes with you; he will never leave you nor forsake
you."
Deuteronomy 31:6

Therefore, since we have been justified through
faith, we have peace with God through our Lord
Jesus Christ,
Romans 5:1

MAY 9

Poetic justice, what will yours be
Where will you spend eternity
Is there a better life for me
If I pick up my cross for Thee

Open my eyes so I can see
How to change and get set free
I come to You on bended knee
Thank You for paying the sinner's fee

But you must return to your God; maintain love
and justice, and wait for your God always.
Hosea 12:6

When justice is done, it brings joy to the righteous but terror to evildoers.
Proverbs 21:15

He has showed you, O man, what is good. And
what does the Lord require of you? To act justly
and to love mercy and to walk humbly with your
God.
Micah 6:8

MAY 10

What a breathtaking site
All the stars in the sky
They are so calming to watch
And I don't know why

Is that what God intended
With each sparkling star
For you to get lost in space
Yet know right where you are

He determines the number of the stars and calls
them each by name.
Psalm 147:4

Those who are wise will shine like the brightness
of the heavens, and those who lead many to righ-
teousness, like the stars for ever and ever.
Daniel 12:3

When I consider your heavens, the work of your
fingers, the moon and the stars, which you have
set in place,
Psalm 8:3

MAY 11

We worry every day
Over everything we do
How do we stop the cycle
And give it all to You

We recognize the problem
Then we turn to You and pray
God give me the strength
To hand this over to You today

Who of you by worrying can add a single hour to his life?

Matthew 6:27

Cast your cares on the Lord and he will sustain you; he will never let the righteous fall.

Psalm 55:22

For nothing is impossible with God."

Luke 1:37

MAY 12

Lord I feel so anxious
I don't know exactly why
Sometimes it gets me so down
I just want to cry

So I stop and pray
For Your comfort and grace
And the ability to trust
Your love in its place

An anxious heart weighs a man down, but a kind word cheers him up.
Proverbs 12:25

Do not be anxious about anything, but in everything, by prayer and petition, with thanksgiving, present your requests to God.
Philippians 4:6

In my anguish I cried to the Lord, and he answered by setting me free.
Psalm 118:5

A new beginning
This year has brought
Look back no more
The past fear not

Moving forward
With each new day
To seek You first
For this I pray

You crown the year with your bounty, and your carts overflow with abundance.
Psalm 65:11

Brothers, I do not consider myself yet to have taken hold of it. But one thing I do: Forgetting what is behind and straining toward what is ahead,
Philippians 3:13

The world and its desires pass away, but the man who does the will of God lives forever.
1 John 2:17

MAY 14

God is never changing
His love and promises are the same
If your relationship is awry
You are to blame

For all through the ages
He has treated us no different
From today back to when
His Son was heaven sent

Jesus Christ is the same yesterday and today and forever.

Hebrews 13:8

God is not a man, that he should lie, nor a son of man, that he should change his mind. Does he speak and then not act? Does he promise and not fulfill?

Numbers 23:19

"I the Lord do not change.

Malachi 3:6

MAY 15

I wish I had their energy
We always say of a child
And yet our God does not grow weary
Isn't that kind of wild

He is available to us
Any time, day or night
With love, support and understanding
He never rests or takes flight

Do you not know? Have you not heard? The Lord is the everlasting God, the Creator of the ends of the earth. He will not grow tired or weary, and his understanding no one can fathom.
Isaiah 40:28

I am with you and will watch over you wherever you go, and I will bring you back to this land. I will not leave you until I have done what I have promised you."
Genesis 28:15

He came to Jesus at night and said, "Rabbi, we know you are a teacher who has come from God. For no one could perform the miraculous signs you are doing if God were not with him."
John 3:2

MAY 16

So many bad things
Happen in this world every day
Sometimes leaving us so sad
And not knowing what to say

Yet we are warned greatly
About the things to come
There is a way to rise above
That is promised to all, not some

There will be great earthquakes, famines and pestilences in various places, and fearful events and great signs from heaven.

Luke 21:11

Now the Spirit expressly says that in later times some will depart from the faith by devoting themselves to deceitful spirits and teachings of demons,

1 Timothy 4:1 (ESV)

Therefore he is able to save completely those who come to God through him, because he always lives to intercede for them.

Hebrews 7:25

MAY 17

If nothing was wrong
With what you did
You would let everyone know
And it wouldn't be hid

It's a lie the devil tells
To try and make you believe
For it is your soul
He means to steal and deceive

The thief comes only to steal and kill and destroy; I have come that they may have life, and have it to the full.

John 10:10

He who conceals his sins does not prosper, but whoever confesses and renounces them finds mercy.

Proverbs 28:13

Woe to those who go to great depths to hide their plans from the Lord, who do their work in darkness and think, "Who sees us? Who will know?"

Isaiah 29:15

MAY 18

Never give up
On the ones you love
You lift them up to God
And trust the One above

To bring healing and truth
In the lives of those lost
Always have faith
Praying continuously at all cost

Therefore, since through God's mercy we have this ministry, we do not lose heart.
2 Corinthians 4:1

Be joyful in hope, patient in affliction, faithful in prayer.
Romans 12:12

pray continually;
1 Thessalonians 5:17

MAY 19

We all have vices
Or strongholds we won't let go
But God gives us a way
This is what we must know

We all have temptations
That we think will not pass
The strength to just say no
Is given if we ask

No temptation has seized you except what is common to man. And God is faithful; he will not let you be tempted beyond what you can bear. But when you are tempted, he will also provide a way out so that you can stand up under it.
1 Corinthians 10:13

The weapons we fight with are not the weapons of the world. On the contrary, they have divine power to demolish strongholds.
2 Corinthians 10:4

But the Lord is faithful, and he will strengthen and protect you from the evil one.
2 Thessalonians 3:3

MAY 20

God's not done with you
And He isn't done with me
We are all in different places
But that's okay you see

For He continues His work
So that each of us can grow
And this never ceases
Until up to heaven we go

being confident of this, that he who began a good work in you will carry it on to completion until the day of Christ Jesus.
Philippians 1:6

Instead, speaking the truth in love, we will in all things grow up into him who is the Head, that is, Christ.
Ephesians 4:15

And we all, with unveiled face, beholding the glory of the Lord, are being transformed into the same image from one degree of glory to another. For this comes from the Lord who is the Spirit.
2 Corinthians 3:18 (ESV)

MAY 21

He is perfect
So we don't have to be
That is a price He paid
Helping to save you and me

I can't imagine how He felt
Showing such love and compassion
To those who took His life
In such a horrible fashion

God made him who had no sin to be sin for us, so that in him we might become the righteousness of God.

2 Corinthians 5:21

who gave himself as a ransom for all men—the testimony given in its proper time.

1 Timothy 2:6

Jesus said, "Father, forgive them, for they do not know what they are doing."

Luke 23:34

MAY 22

Give your best to God
He gives His best to you
From sending us His only Son
To helping us in everything we do

He doesn't say I will try
What He says He makes it true
So do the same for Him
To build His faith in you

Whatever you do, work at it with all your heart,
as working for the Lord, not for men,
Colossians 3:23

Every good and perfect gift is from above, com-
ing down from the Father of the heavenly lights,
who does not change like shifting shadows.
James 1:17

"His master replied, 'Well done, good and faith-
ful servant! You have been faithful with a few
things; I will put you in charge of many things.
Come and share your master's happiness!'
Matthew 25:21

Have a faith that listens to God
If you believe in Him, yet do not follow
How is that a life fulfilled
This will only leave you hollow

Ask for His will in your life
Trust the guidance in His word
Actively live out your faith
It is more than repeating what you've heard

Whatever you have learned or received or heard from me, or seen in me—put it into practice. And the God of peace will be with you.

Philippians 4:9

The man who says, "I know him," but does not do what he commands is a liar, and the truth is not in him.

1 John 2:4

What good is it, my brothers, if a man claims to have faith but has no deeds?

James 2:14

MAY 24

Faith lived outside of obedience
Is not pleasing to our God
For if we truly love and adore Him
Shouldn't we give Him more than a nod

If He is invited into our heart
That creates a desire to please
Making us want to do the right thing
Which isn't always done with ease

Love the Lord your God and keep his require-
ments, his decrees, his laws and his commands
always.

Deuteronomy 11:1

We demolish arguments and every pretension
that sets itself up against the knowledge of God,
and we take captive every thought to make it
obedient to Christ.

2 Corinthians 10:5

As obedient children, do not conform to the evil
desires you had when you lived in ignorance.

1 Peter 1:14

MAY 25

Our life is full of many people
That are important and we love
Yet if we don't put God first
We are never straight with Him above

For if God is our main focus
He ensures everything else will be in place
We will be better prepared for others
And able to serve them with love and grace

But seek first his kingdom and his righteousness,
and all these things will be given to you as well.
Matthew 6:33

Finally, brothers, we instructed you how to live
in order to please God, as in fact you are living.
Now we ask you and urge you in the Lord Jesus
to do this more and more.
1 Thessalonians 4:1

who comforts us in all our troubles, so that we
can comfort those in any trouble with the com-
fort we ourselves have received from God.
2 Corinthians 1:4

When you give to God first
He fills the rest in
Whether it's tithes, time or love
Your end is where He will begin

When you give to God last
If you have anything left
It robs you both of a blessing
Being the worst kind of theft

Remember this: Whoever sows sparingly will also reap sparingly, and whoever sows generously will also reap generously.

2 Corinthians 9:6

One man gives freely, yet gains even more; another withholds unduly, but comes to poverty.

Proverbs 11:24

Give, and it will be given to you. A good measure, pressed down, shaken together and running over, will be poured into your lap. For with the measure you use, it will be measured to you."

Luke 6:38

MAY 27

When you think there is only one way
To drown your heartache and pain
Let me tell you of another
That gives you much more than comfort to gain

His name is Jesus Christ
He lived, died and rose again for you
And if not thinking of your hurt is the goal
It is that and so much more He can do

"Be careful, or your hearts will be weighed down with dissipation, drunkenness and the anxieties of life, and that day will close on you unexpectedly like a trap.
Luke 21:34

It is for freedom that Christ has set us free. Stand firm, then, and do not let yourselves be burdened again by a yoke of slavery.
Galatians 5:1

It is because of the Lord's lovingkindnesses that we are not consumed, because His compassions never fail.
Lamentations 3:22 (AMP)

MAY 28

As I get more into His word
My heart seems to overflow
And as my heart fills
It increases my desire to grow

It's a wonderful circle
That I love going around
One feeds the other
Making my faith abound

My lips will shout for joy when I sing praise to
you—I, whom you have redeemed.
Psalm 71:23

When your words came, I ate them; they were
my joy and my heart's delight, for I bear your
name, O Lord God Almighty.
Jeremiah 15:16

The precepts of the Lord are right, giving joy to
the heart. The commands of the Lord are radi-
ant, giving light to the eyes.
Psalm 19:8

MAY 29

Maybe it's a candy bar
Or just one more drink
We all have things we turn to
Trying not to think

To push down the pain
Of what we can't let go
But the void just grows
As long as we try to run the show

Wine is a mocker and beer a brawler; whoever is led astray by them is not wise.

Proverbs 20:1

"Forget the former things; do not dwell on the past.

Isaiah 43:18

Submit yourselves, then, to God. Resist the devil, and he will flee from you.

James 4:7

MAY 30

There are so many
Full of anger and pain
Feeling so unworthy
Of any positive gain

But there is one
That can take that all away
He loves and cares for you
And seeks you every day

Humble yourselves before the Lord, and he will lift you up.

James 4:10

Get rid of all bitterness, rage and anger, brawling and slander, along with every form of malice.

Ephesians 4:31

Since you are precious and honored in my sight, and because I love you, I will give men in exchange for you, and people in exchange for your life.

Isaiah 43:4

MAY 31

If we each shared a blessing
With someone that we knew
Could that change the life
Of them or of you

Be mindful of others needs
And if there is something you can do
You never know what it will mean to them
Or how much blessing it will be to you

Give generously to him and do so without a
grudging heart; then because of this the Lord
your God will bless you in all your work and in
everything you put your hand to.

Deuteronomy 15:10

In all things I have shown you that by working
hard in this way we must help the weak and
remember the words of the Lord Jesus, how he
himself said, 'It is more blessed to give than to
receive.'"

Acts 20:35 (ESV)

Do not withhold good from those who deserve
it, when it is in your power to act.

Proverbs 3:27

JUNE 1

So much of my life I wasted
My priorities were all wrong
Not that I led a bad life
For a relationship with God I did long

Yet from the day I started that journey
And let Jesus into my heart
I have grown in love and grace
From Him I will never part

Blessed is the man who finds wisdom, the man who gains understanding,
$\qquad$ Proverbs 3:13

But grow in the grace and knowledge of our Lord and Savior Jesus Christ. To him be glory both now and forever! Amen.
$\qquad$ 2 Peter 3:18

May the Lord make your love increase and overflow for each other and for everyone else, just as ours does for you.
$\qquad$ 1 Thessalonians 3:12

JUNE 2

There is not one question
That can't be answered by His word
You only need to look
And actually hear what you've heard

Meditate and pray on your answer
Apply His word to your situation
For He will not leave you helpless
As you are His greatest creation

"Ask and it will be given to you; seek and you will find; knock and the door will be opened to you.
Matthew 7:7

'Call to me and I will answer you and tell you great and unsearchable things you do not know.'
Jeremiah 33:3

If any of you lacks wisdom, he should ask God, who gives generously to all without finding fault, and it will be given to him.
James 1:5

JUNE 3

We are each beautiful
In our own special way
Like the snowflakes in the sky
On a cold winter's day

Some are big, some are small
They might be plain or pretty as a flower
Each unique, yet all the same
Loved by Him every minute of every hour

I praise you because I am fearfully and wonder-
fully made; your works are wonderful, I know
that full well.

Psalm 139:14

Yet, O Lord, you are our Father. We are the clay,
you are the potter; we are all the work of your
hand.

Isaiah 64:8

But the Lord said to Samuel, "Do not consider
his appearance or his height, for I have rejected
him. The Lord does not look at the things man
looks at. Man looks at the outward appearance,
but the Lord looks at the heart."

1 Samuel 16:7

JUNE 4

You are not your circumstance
For it is ever changing all around
It should not affect your inner core
If that's where Christ does abound

He is never changing and true
And the caretaker of my soul
So while everything around me is awry
My spirit will not take a toll

Jesus Christ is the same yesterday and today and forever.

Hebrews 13:8

If we are thrown into the blazing furnace, the God we serve is able to save us from it, and he will rescue us from your hand, O King.

Daniel 3:17

Yet I am poor and needy; may the Lord think of me. You are my help and my deliverer; O my God, do not delay.

Psalm 40:17

JUNE 5

As I set and listen
To the windchimes sing
It transports my mind
Away to soothing things

To times and places
That are near and far
Reminding me of the peace
You give no matter where we are

The Lord gives strength to his people; the Lord blesses his people with peace.

Psalm 29:11

You will go out in joy and be led forth in peace; the mountains and hills will burst into song before you, and all the trees of the field will clap their hands.

Isaiah 55:12

Now may the Lord of peace himself give you peace at all times and in every way. The Lord be with all of you.

2 Thessalonians 3:16

JUNE 6

If you say, "I'll pray for you."
Be sure you follow through
It blesses the one in need
And makes your words ring true

So take a moment right then
And lift up your fellow man
For if you put it off until later
It may not cross your mind again

I urge, then, first of all, that requests, prayers, intercession and thanksgiving be made for everyone—

1 Timothy 2:1

And the Lord restored the fortunes of Job, when he had prayed for his friends. And the Lord gave Job twice as much as he had before.

Job 42:10 (ESV)

And pray in the Spirit on all occasions with all kinds of prayers and requests. With this in mind, be alert and always keep on praying for all the saints.

Ephesians 6:18

JUNE 7

Not everyone was born with a silver spoon
Yet we were all given a silver tongue
And whether that silver is tarnished or shines
Is something we start learning while we are young

For it is the greatest instrument
You will learn to use in your life
Bringing joy, love and kindness to this world
Or spreading despair, heartache and strife

Reckless words pierce like a sword, but the tongue of the wise brings healing.
Proverbs 12:18

Let no corrupting talk come out of your mouths, but only such as is good for building up, as fits the occasion, that it may give grace to those who hear.
Ephesians 4:29 (ESV)

"Whoever desires to love life and see good days, let him keep his tongue from evil and his lips from speaking deceit;
1 Peter 3:10 (ESV)

JUNE 8

There is not enough time in a day
And time is given great value
Be careful how you spend time
For losing time could cost you

When you have too much time on your hands
Your time could be easily wasted
So follow Him who has stood the test of time
For that time would be wisely invested

making the best use of the time, because the days
are evil.

Ephesians 5:16 (ESV)

He has made everything beautiful in its time. He
has also set eternity in the hearts of men; yet they
cannot fathom what God has done from begin-
ning to end.

Ecclesiastes 3:11

"I the Lord do not change.

Malachi 3:6

JUNE 9

God is like the wind
You cannot see either per se
But you can watch what they move
In a powerful mighty way

The rustling of the leaves
Or in an answered prayer
You don't have to see the force behind
To know what is there

The wind blows wherever it pleases. You hear its sound, but you cannot tell where it comes from or where it is going. So it is with everyone born of the Spirit."

John 3:8

He who forms the mountains, creates the wind, and reveals his thoughts to man, he who turns dawn to darkness, and treads the high places of the earth—the Lord God Almighty is his name.

Amos 4:13

Before they call I will answer; while they are still speaking I will hear.

Isaiah 65:24

JUNE 10

Everyone says your either a follower or leader
I say as a child of God you are both
You are to follow God where He leads
But also lead by example is part of your oath

To be a good leader of the faith
You must be a good follower of God
Making us a good blend of both
Any other explanation seems odd

"Come, follow me," Jesus said, "and I will make you fishers of men."
Matthew 4:19

To this you were called, because Christ suffered for you, leaving you an example, that you should follow in his steps.
1 Peter 2:21

even as I try to please everybody in every way. For I am not seeking my own good but the good of many, so that they may be saved. Follow my example, as I follow the example of Christ.
1 Corinthians 10:33

JUNE 11

What does good listening require
It means you must be willing to hear
To let someone pour their heart out
Without any judgement or fear

You should share their joy or their pain
Not the words they entrusted to you
Pray with your friend in need
And together ask God what to do

Therefore confess your sins to each other and pray for each other so that you may be healed. The prayer of a righteous man is powerful and effective.

James 5:16

A gossip betrays a confidence, but a trustworthy man keeps a secret.

Proverbs 11:13

He who answers before listening—that is his folly and his shame.

Proverbs 18:13

JUNE 12

Everyone makes a difference
In someone that you know
How you live your life
Decides which way that difference will go

So try to live your life right
Be thoughtful in what you do and say
For you are planting a seed
That might save someone's life some day

Don't let anyone look down on you because you are young, but set an example for the believers in speech, in life, in love, in faith and in purity.
1 Timothy 4:12

Train a child in the way he should go, and when he is old he will not turn from it.
Proverbs 22:6

The unfolding of your words gives light; it gives understanding to the simple.
Psalm 119:130

We are joyous in the Lord
So others will see the light
Shining from within us
This is precious in His sight

For when we give the glory to God
In all we say or do
It opens up our soul
Allowing Him to shine through

Not to us, O Lord, not to us but to your name be the glory, because of your love and faithfulness.
Psalm 115:1

For this is what the Lord has commanded us: "'I have made you a light for the Gentiles, that you may bring salvation to the ends of the earth.'"
Acts 13:47

"No one lights a lamp and hides it in a jar or puts it under a bed. Instead, he puts it on a stand, so that those who come in can see the light.
Luke 8:16

JUNE 14

With friends that support bad habits
Who needs enemies around
I thought friends were to lift you up
Not hold you to the ground

They are to make you accountable with love
Not jump right in and go down too
You need to wake up and realize
What a friend is and what they are to do

If one falls down, his friend can help him up. But pity the man who falls and has no one to help him up!

Ecclesiastes 4:10

Brothers, if someone is caught in a sin, you who are spiritual should restore him gently. But watch yourself, or you also may be tempted.

Galatians 6:1

Blessed are the peacemakers, for they will be called sons of God.

Matthew 5:9

JUNE 15

When you have a close circle
Yet deep down it doesn't feel right
Are they really who you should be around
Do they pray for you each night

Or do they speak what you want to hear
And do the things you want done
Is the circle you are surrounded with
There to please you or God's Son

Therefore each of you must put off falsehood and speak truthfully to his neighbor, for we are all members of one body.
                    Ephesians 4:25

He who walks with the wise grows wise, but a companion of fools suffers harm.
                    Proverbs 13:20

But if we walk in the light, as he is in the light, we have fellowship with one another, and the blood of Jesus, his Son, purifies us from all sin.
                    1 John 1:7

JUNE 16

Do you ever feel trapped
And keep doing the same thing wrong
You want to change what you're doing
Yet don't believe you are that strong

Well if you're trying alone, you're right
There is only one who can break the sin
And together you can move that mountain
If you repent and turn to Him

He replied, "Because you have so little faith. I tell you the truth, if you have faith as small as a mustard seed, you can say to this mountain, 'Move from here to there' and it will move. Nothing will be impossible for you."
Matthew 17:20

For I take no pleasure in the death of anyone, declares the Sovereign Lord. Repent and live!
Ezekiel 18:32

I do not understand what I do. For what I want to do I do not do, but what I hate I do.
Romans 7:15

JUNE 17

Don't let feelings of failure, guilt or shame
Keep you down and in the dark
Those are lies the devil tells
So you will stay under his mark

You have a God that loves you
Regardless of what you have done
He is waiting to give you light
With Him your victory will be won

For the Lord your God is the one who goes with
you to fight for you against your enemies to give
you victory."
Deuteronomy 20:4

But the Lord is faithful, and he will strengthen
and protect you from the evil one.
2 Thessalonians 3:3

To you they cried and were rescued; in you they
trusted and were not put to shame.
Psalm 22:5 (ESV)

JUNE 18

When someone asks for prayer
And shares the reason why
It should burden your heart for them
Don't let the opportunity pass by

Show them compassion and kindness
Lift up their needs when you pray
The reason is not your concern
Just give them to God today

Be devoted to one another in brotherly love.
Honor one another above yourselves.
Romans 12:10

This is the confidence we have in approaching
God: that if we ask anything according to his
will, he hears us.
1 John 5:14

Brothers, pray for us.
1 Thessalonians 5:25

JUNE 19

Do you need constant encouragement
To help you make it through
Is that a direct link
In the self-confidence in you

Try looking closer at God
And the confidence He will provide
For if you are a child of His
In His will be confident and do not hide

For God did not give us a spirit of timidity, but a spirit of power, of love and of self-discipline.
2 Timothy 1:7

So do not throw away your confidence; it will be richly rewarded. You need to persevere so that when you have done the will of God, you will receive what he has promised.
Hebrews 10:35–36

for the Lord will be your confidence and will keep your foot from being snared.
Proverbs 3:26

JUNE 20

Being strong and courageous
Doesn't mean going in blind
You must be focused on God
To be in your right frame of mind

You were made for greatness
Not to be obtained on your own
Try hard not to compare your success
It is only you that reaps what you've sewn

Have I not commanded you? Be strong and courageous. Do not be terrified; do not be discouraged, for the Lord your God will be with you wherever you go."

Joshua 1:9

"Do not be afraid, O man highly esteemed," he said. "Peace! Be strong now; be strong." When he spoke to me, I was strengthened and said, "Speak, my lord, since you have given me strength."

Daniel 10:19

You then, my son, be strong in the grace that is in Christ Jesus.

2 Timothy 2:1

JUNE 21

Blessings from people
Are gifts from above
They are driven to help you
Because of God's love

So accept them with care
Be thankful and pray
That you follow those blessings
And that God shows you the way

And do not forget to do good and to share with others, for with such sacrifices God is pleased.
Hebrews 13:16

Each of you should look not only to your own interests, but also to the interests of others.
Philippians 2:4

In him we were also chosen, having been predestined according to the plan of him who works out everything in conformity with the purpose of his will,
Ephesians 1:11

We all have a desire
To make others proud
But our aim should be higher
Than our earthly thoughts allowed

For once we are saved
And follow God's commands
The recognition we craved
From others no longer stands

Am I now trying to win the approval of men, or of God? Or am I trying to please men? If I were still trying to please men, I would not be a servant of Christ.

Galatians 1:10

How can you believe if you accept praise from one another, yet make no effort to obtain the praise that comes from the only God?

John 5:44

Peter and the other apostles replied: "We must obey God rather than men!

Acts 5:29

JUNE 23

There are so many things
We say stand in our way
Are the obstacles actually there
Or is it just something we say

Maybe they really are
To get us back on track
Because we took off on our own
For His will we did lack

I will instruct you and teach you in the way you should go; I will counsel you with my eye upon you.

Psalm 32:8 (ESV)

but whoever listens to me will dwell secure and will be at ease, without dread of disaster."

Proverbs 1:33 (ESV)

Therefore do not be foolish, but understand what the Lord's will is.

Ephesians 5:17

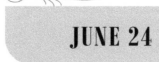

We never know the pain
Someone else may feel
What they actually go through
Or how well they can deal

That reminds us the importance
Of always being kind
To help each other when we can
For we don't know their frame of mind

Be kind and compassionate to one another, for-giving each other, just as in Christ God forgave you.

Ephesians 4:32

Finally, all of you, live in harmony with one another; be sympathetic, love as brothers, be compassionate and humble.

1 Peter 3:8

Therefore, as God's chosen people, holy and dearly loved, clothe yourselves with compassion, kindness, humility, gentleness and patience.

Colossians 3:12

JUNE 25

Life lessons can be hard
Yet are necessary to grow
Try to figure out their meaning
But onward you must go

They are part of our big picture
That we are not able to see
But He makes it all for our good
We need only to trust in Thee

Trust in the Lord with all your heart and lean not on your own understanding; in all your ways acknowledge him, and he will make your paths straight.

Proverbs 3:5–6

Consider it pure joy, my brothers, whenever you face trials of many kinds, because you know that the testing of your faith develops perseverance.

James 1:2–3

And we know that in all things God works for the good of those who love him, who have been called according to his purpose.

Romans 8:28

JUNE 26

When you are loaded with fear and doubt
Don't turn away from your God
And try to resolve things on your own
Making your faith seem like a fraud

You know He is there for you
And in Him you trust and believe
Remember He is there at all times
Not just when you choose to receive

"Why do you call me, 'Lord, Lord,' and do not do what I say?
                    Luke 6:46

Have I not commanded you? Be strong and courageous. Do not be terrified; do not be discouraged, for the Lord your God will be with you wherever you go."
                    Joshua 1:9

The Lord is compassionate and gracious, slow to anger, abounding in love.
                    Psalm 103:8

JUNE 27

When you feel the walls are caving in
Reach out to someone you love
And don't forget the Good Father
Sent to you from above

He is the best strong tower
To protect you when you fall
He is always there for you
With comfort and mercy through it all

and call upon me in the day of trouble; I will
deliver you, and you will honor me."
Psalm 50:15

but those who hope in the Lord will renew their
strength. They will soar on wings like eagles; they
will run and not grow weary, they will walk and
not be faint.
Isaiah 40:31

The name of the Lord is a strong tower; the righ-
teous run to it and are safe.
Proverbs 18:10

JUNE 28

Our God is a God of promises
He is a God that keeps His word
There is nothing He won't do for you
Not a cry out He hasn't heard

Give your heart to Him
No better gift will you ever receive
Than the love and grace He will bestow
There are no tricks up His sleeve

He who did not spare his own Son, but gave him
up for us all—how will he not also, along with
him, graciously give us all things?
Romans 8:32

"Praise be to the Lord, who has given rest to
his people Israel just as he promised. Not one
word has failed of all the good promises he gave
through his servant Moses.
1 Kings 8:56

in hope of eternal life, which God, who never
lies, promised before the ages began
Titus 1:2 (ESV)

JUNE 29

Our God is an awesome God
He never ceases to amaze
His love abounds in me
Him I will forever praise

I will lift His name on high
His living water I will drink
To be so overwhelmed by His spirit
That I can hardly think

Praise the Lord. How good it is to sing praises to our God, how pleasant and fitting to praise him!
Psalm 147:1

On the last day of the feast, the great day, Jesus stood up and cried out, "If anyone thirsts, let him come to me and drink. Whoever believes in me, as the Scripture has said, 'Out of his heart will flow rivers of living water.'"
John 7:37–38 (ESV)

Do not get drunk on wine, which leads to debauchery. Instead, be filled with the Spirit.
Ephesians 5:18

JUNE 30

There is so much more to sight
Than just the ability to look around
It should invoke your emotions
To see that which cannot be found

Yet if it's not seen with our eyes
Does that make it unable to find
For we are surrounded by love, hope and faith
And these are the ties that bind

So we fix our eyes not on what is seen, but on what is unseen. For what is seen is temporary, but what is unseen is eternal.

2 Corinthians 4:18

And now these three remain: faith, hope and love. But the greatest of these is love.

1 Corinthians 13:13

Hear this, you foolish and senseless people, who have eyes but do not see, who have ears but do not hear:

Jeremiah 5:21

JULY 1

God has a special way
Of making everything fall into place
It's all part of His design
And His amazing grace

It isn't by chance or karma
Or some freaky coincidence
But the predestined plan for you
And your eternal inheritance

your eyes saw my unformed body. All the days
ordained for me were written in your book before
one of them came to be.

Psalm 139:16

A man's steps are directed by the Lord. How then
can anyone understand his own way?

Proverbs 20:24

For we are God's workmanship, created in Christ
Jesus to do good works, which God prepared in
advance for us to do.

Ephesians 2:10

JULY 2

We make time for ourselves
For our family, friends or spouse
And on Sunday morning
We even make it to God's house

God gave us His only Son
As the ultimate sacrifice
Shouldn't we dedicate our life to Him
Just a little time won't suffice

Therefore, I urge you, brothers, in view of God's mercy, to offer your bodies as living sacrifices, holy and pleasing to God—this is your spiritual act of worship.

Romans 12:1

Love the Lord your God with all your heart and with all your soul and with all your strength.

Deuteronomy 6:5

Don't you know that you yourselves are God's temple and that God's Spirit lives in you?

1 Corinthians 3:16

JULY 3

Who am I to judge another
Or to point out every time they sin
For it is the Lord that is to judge
He will do that at our life's end

We are here to lift each other up
With love and prayer keep straight our path
To show a good example with our life in Christ
And lessen the need of our Lord's wrath

There is only one Lawgiver and Judge, the one who is able to save and destroy. But you—who are you to judge your neighbor?
James 4:12

Each of us should please his neighbor for his good, to build him up.
Romans 15:2

For by your words you will be acquitted, and by your words you will be condemned."
Matthew 12:37

JULY 4

What joy it brings me
To sing my heart's desire
Whether around the house
Or singing in the choir

Find the praise you like
That brings joy to you
I assure you it pleases God
When you let Him shine through

The Lord is my strength and my song; he has become my salvation. He is my God, and I will praise him, my father's God, and I will exalt him.
Exodus 15:2

Worship the Lord with gladness; come before him with joyful songs.
Psalm 100:2

For you were once darkness, but now you are light in the Lord. Live as children of light
Ephesians 5:8

JULY 5

Some people don't understand
The hurt they put others through
They think it only hurts them
No matter what they do

As followers of Jesus Christ
Our hearts go out to them
We feel their joy and pain
For we have learned how to love from Him

Rejoice with those who rejoice; mourn with those who mourn.
Romans 12:15

Carry each other's burdens, and in this way you will fulfill the law of Christ.
Galatians 6:2

If one part suffers, every part suffers with it; if one part is honored, every part rejoices with it.
1 Corinthians 12:26

JULY 6

When you feel you are not enough
And the things of this world have you down
Don't allow your faith to become empty words
And take away the glory of His crown

For our God is a God of love
He never once will abandon your side
Open your heart and accept His mercy
Humble yourself and swallow your pride

Humble yourselves, therefore, under God's
mighty hand, that he may lift you up in due time.
1 Peter 5:6

Whatever you have learned or received or heard
from me, or seen in me—put it into practice.
And the God of peace will be with you.
Philippians 4:9

When pride comes, then comes disgrace, but
with humility comes wisdom.
Proverbs 11:2

JULY 7

There are so many in this world
That don't feel acceptance or love
They have no idea and can't conceive
What was sent to them from above

Pay attention to those around you
Share with them God's love and grace
They are lost yet can be found
Finding comfort with their eternal place

My command is this: Love each other as I have
loved you.

John 15:12

For there is no difference between Jew and
Gentile—the same Lord is Lord of all and richly
blesses all who call on him,

Romans 10:12

"A new command I give you: Love one another.
As I have loved you, so you must love one another.

John 13:34

JULY 8

Do you get up each morning
Feeling your life is mundane
And if something doesn't change
It might drive you insane

Maybe it's not a change of scenery
But a change in your outlook
For if your routine was to glorify God
You would be living proof of the good book

I will always obey your law, for ever and ever.
Psalm 119:44

And whatever you do, whether in word or deed, do it all in the name of the Lord Jesus, giving thanks to God the Father through him.
Colossians 3:17

Are you so foolish? After beginning with the Spirit, are you now trying to attain your goal by human effort?
Galatians 3:3

JULY 9

Do you ever feel selfish
Like you have so much more to give
But you don't want to give up your time
Or how you like to live

Well that is the Holy Spirit
Tugging away at your heart
And if you want your life fulfilled
You need to figure it out and where to start

He who is kind to the poor lends to the Lord,
and he will reward him for what he has done.
Proverbs 19:17

As has just been said: "Today, if you hear his
voice, do not harden your hearts as you did in
the rebellion."
Hebrews 3:15

And all these blessings shall come upon you and
overtake you, if you obey the voice of the Lord
your God.
Deuteronomy 28:2 (ESV)

JULY 10

Freedom is so desired
For no-one wants to be bound
What is freedom to you
Where can it be found

It's really not a physical place
Like you imagine it to be
Just give your heart to God
Your freedom will be eternity

It is for freedom that Christ has set us free. Stand firm, then, and do not let yourselves be burdened again by a yoke of slavery.

Galatians 5:1

that the creation itself will be set free from its bondage to corruption and obtain the freedom of the glory of the children of God.

Romans 8:21 (ESV)

Then you will know the truth, and the truth will set you free."

John 8:32

JULY 11

If God told you to build an ark
Would you follow through
There are things He asks of us
That we will never do

Because it's not life or death
Requests from Him seem small
Ignoring Him reflects our faith
What will you do with His call

By faith Noah, when warned about things not yet seen, in holy fear built an ark to save his family. By his faith he condemned the world and became heir of the righteousness that comes by faith.

Hebrews 11:7

"And if you faithfully obey the voice of the Lord your God, being careful to do all his commandments that I command you today, the Lord your God will set you high above all the nations of the earth.

Deuteronomy 28:1 (ESV)

For you have need of endurance, so that when you have done the will of God you may receive what is promised.

Hebrews 10:36 (ESV)

JULY 12

Why wait to access your beliefs
Until something in your life goes wrong
Then you cry out to God in need
Knowing when you are weak He is strong

How much better would your life be
If you lived what you believe every day
So that when those trials come along
They don't fill you with such dismay

Now the Bereans were of more noble character than the Thessalonians, for they received the message with great eagerness and examined the Scriptures every day to see if what Paul said was true.

Acts 17:11

Seek the Lord and his strength; seek his presence continually!

Psalm 105:4 (ESV)

Live as free men, but do not use your freedom as a cover-up for evil; live as servants of God.

1 Peter 2:16

JULY 13

Don't just go to church on Sunday
Be the church seven days a week
Live your life knowing that one day
You will meet the One you seek

He won't want to hear your excuses
Or ask any reasons why
He will look at your heart and it's uses
So don't just let your Sunday go by

What good is it, my brothers, if a man claims to
have faith but has no deeds?

James 2:14

Live such good lives among the pagans that,
though they accuse you of doing wrong, they
may see your good deeds and glorify God on the
day he visits us.

1 Peter 2:12

"I the Lord search the heart and examine the
mind, to reward a man according to his conduct,
according to what his deeds deserve."

Jeremiah 17:10

JULY 14

Who you surround yourself with matters
It's not just an old wives' tale
They can drag you down to the gutter
Or help your life set sail

Birds of a feather flock together
And God's sheep should too
There's nothing worse than being a turkey
When it's so much better to be a ewe!

Have nothing to do with godless myths and old wives' tales; rather, train yourself to be godly.
1 Timothy 4:7

Do not be misled: "Bad company corrupts good character."
1 Corinthians 15:33

Know that the Lord is God. It is he who made us, and we are his; we are his people, the sheep of his pasture.
Psalm 100:3

JULY 15

If we can't explore the oceans deepest depths
And the space surrounding our world has no end
Then why can't we wrap our minds around
The overwhelming wonders of God that do not bend

For we believe what we don't see in the ocean blue
And understand the concept of time and space
Yet continually question the very God
That put all of these things into place

In the beginning God created the heavens and the earth.

Genesis 1:1

How many are your works, O Lord! In wisdom you made them all; the earth is full of your creatures.

Psalm 104:24

Ignoring what they said, Jesus told the synagogue ruler, "Don't be afraid; just believe."

Mark 5:36

JULY 16

God is everywhere all at once
He knows everything at all times
He has the ability of unlimited types of creation
He is our absolute in ultimate paradigms

The love of our God abounds like no other
There are so many words to describe Him
Omnipotent, omnificent, omnipresent
Omniscient and omnibenevolent bring it all in

Great is our Lord and mighty in power; his
understanding has no limit.
Psalm 147:5

Can anyone hide in secret places so that I cannot
see him?" declares the Lord. "Do not I fill heaven
and earth?" declares the Lord.
Jeremiah 23:24

whenever our hearts condemn us. For God is
greater than our hearts, and he knows everything.
1 John 3:20

JULY 17

Everything we take with us is full
Shouldn't we treat ourselves with the same respect
For we wouldn't tote around an empty purse
Or fly with an empty suitcase to inspect

What would the point of an empty cup be
Or a car with no gas or flat tires
It's time to fill your heart with God's love
And stop living in empty earthly desires

I will give you a new heart and put a new spirit in you; I will remove from you your heart of stone and give you a heart of flesh.
Ezekiel 36:26

let us draw near to God with a sincere heart in full assurance of faith, having our hearts sprinkled to cleanse us from a guilty conscience and having our bodies washed with pure water.
Hebrews 10:22

I have stored up your word in my heart, that I might not sin against you.
Psalm 119:11 (ESV)

JULY 18

How come when we do something wrong
We can't just admit it and confess
For by diverting actions and blame
We can turn something small into a mess

We know what we did was wrong
Take ownership and face the consequences
Humble ourselves and swallow our pride
And stop living under false pretenses

Turn my heart toward your statutes and not
toward selfish gain.
Psalm 119:36

having a form of godliness but denying its power.
Have nothing to do with them.
2 Timothy 3:5

Then I will go back to my place until they admit
their guilt. And they will seek my face; in their
misery they will earnestly seek me."
Hosea 5:15

JULY 19

If we do something because it's the right thing
Does that make it void of love
For love is the greatest commandment
Of our Heavenly Father from above

I think if we do what His will says
And have prayed to come to that conclusion
Then it's full of love to please Him
Making the right thing and love a perfect infusion

"A new command I give you: Love one another.
As I have loved you, so you must love one another.
John 13:34

Do everything in love.
1 Corinthians 16:14

Dear children, let us not love with words or
tongue but with actions and in truth.
1 John 3:18

JULY 20

Today is a day of wonders
It is a day of tremendous joy
What is so special today, you ask
I'm treating my faith like a new toy!

Remember when you were a kid
The excitement of something new
Well that feeling can be yours today
Depending on your point of view

Rejoice in the Lord always. I will say it again: Rejoice!

Philippians 4:4

This is the day the Lord has made; let us rejoice and be glad in it.

Psalm 118:24

You will go out in joy and be led forth in peace; the mountains and hills will burst into song before you, and all the trees of the field will clap their hands.

Isaiah 55:12

JULY 21

They say everything has a silver lining
Sometimes you must look hard but it's there
When one door closes another will open
You need only walk through if you dare

So don't sit around in self pity
There is so much more to gain
Look for the possibilities of your situation
Lift it up in prayer and let God ease the pain

give thanks in all circumstances, for this is God's
will for you in Christ Jesus.
1 Thessalonians 5:18

A cheerful heart is good medicine, but a crushed
spirit dries up the bones.
Proverbs 17:22

Blessed is the man who perseveres under trial,
because when he has stood the test, he will receive
the crown of life that God has promised to those
who love him.
James 1:12

JULY 22

If God can part the Red Sea
Then what can He not do for you
He can put you where you need to be
And help you do that which you need to do

So give up your fear and anxiety
In the things you have left undone
Trust in the One that loves you faithfully
And give control to the Promised One

Then Moses stretched out his hand over the sea, and all that night the Lord drove the sea back with a strong east wind and turned it into dry land. The waters were divided,
Exodus 14:21

Stretch out your hand to heal and perform miraculous signs and wonders through the name of your holy servant Jesus."
Acts 4:30

You are the God who performs miracles; you display your power among the peoples.
Psalm 77:14

When someone does you wrong
You must forgive and let it go
If you don't do these things
They are forever in control

So set yourself free
From the pain they have inflicted
End your constant thoughts of them
And the control will be shifted

But I tell you: Love your enemies and pray for those who persecute you,
Matthew 5:44

"Do not judge, and you will not be judged. Do not condemn, and you will not be condemned. Forgive, and you will be forgiven.
Luke 6:37

And when you stand praying, if you hold anything against anyone, forgive him, so that your Father in heaven may forgive you your sins."
Mark 11:25

JULY 24

God gives us so many things to help
With struggles we face every day
We need to use them and be thankful
And listen to what He is trying to say

So whether it be a friend with advice
A smile from a stranger on the street
Fleeting thoughts on a direction to go
Watch for them both, big or discrete

God also testified to it by signs, wonders and various miracles, and gifts of the Holy Spirit distributed according to his will.
                          Hebrews 2:4

And they went out and preached everywhere, while the Lord worked with them and confirmed the message by accompanying signs.
                    Mark 16:20 (ESV)

They performed his miraculous signs among them, his wonders in the land of Ham.
                         Psalm 105:27

When something is wonderful
Does it fill you with wonder
Which can take your breath away
The beauty cannot be held under

Or does it invoke a different feeling
Does it fill you with wonder
Which can make you desire to know more
Leaving its creation to ponder

Everyone was filled with awe, and many wonders and miraculous signs were done by the apostles.

Acts 2:43

they flowed over the mountains, they went down into the valleys, to the place you assigned for them.

Psalm 104:8

This is what God the Lord says—he who created the heavens and stretched them out, who spread out the earth and all that comes out of it, who gives breath to its people, and life to those who walk on it:

Isaiah 42:5

JULY 26

Is it always a bad thing
To add fuel to the fire
Not in regard to your soul
If it is God you desire

Be careful of the fuel you use
To make your fire grow
It should be faith, hope and love
To achieve that inner glow

Do not put out the Spirit's fire;
1 Thessalonians 5:19

Why are you downcast, O my soul? Why so disturbed within me? Put your hope in God, for I will yet praise him, my Savior and my God.
Psalm 42:11

But be very careful to keep the commandment and the law that Moses the servant of the Lord gave you: to love the Lord your God, to walk in all his ways, to obey his commands, to hold fast to him and to serve him with all your heart and all your soul."
Joshua 22:5

JULY 27

Out of all the noise around me
I choose to voluntarily hear
Why do I not listen to God
As He speaks gently in my ear

He is the only thing
That is always in perfect tune
I need to block out the racket and listen
For it's my heart He is trying to hewn

"Consider carefully what you hear," he continued. "With the measure you use, it will be measured to you—and even more.
Mark 4:24

Here I am! I stand at the door and knock. If anyone hears my voice and opens the door, I will come in and eat with him, and he with me.
Revelation 3:20

Moreover, he said to me, "Son of man, all my words that I shall speak to you receive in your heart, and hear with your ears.
Ezekiel 3:10 (ESV)

JULY 28

Can you truly imagine
Being in the presence of our Lord
It will be more glorious
Than anything you have seen or heard

Emotion will overtake you
Never such love will you feel
You won't have a clear thought
Except to bow down and kneel

It is written: "'As surely as I live,' says the Lord, 'every knee will bow before me; every tongue will confess to God.'"

Romans 14:11

But, as it is written, "What no eye has seen, nor ear heard, nor the heart of man imagined, what God has prepared for those who love him."

1 Corinthians 2:9 (ESV)

I, John, am the one who heard and saw these things. And when I had heard and seen them, I fell down to worship at the feet of the angel who had been showing them to me.

Revelation 22:8

It says to be imitators of Christ
What does that actually mean
How do we imitate someone
We have never literally seen

You begin with believing in Him
And asking Him into your heart
Then daily dive into His word
Your imitation will begin to start

We live by faith, not by sight.
2 Corinthians 5:7

No one has ever seen God; but if we love one another, God lives in us and his love is made complete in us.
1 John 4:12

Whoever claims to live in him must walk as Jesus did.
1 John 2:6

JULY 30

Sometimes do you feel numb inside
Your hearts defense against all the wrong
There is a different way to react
That will leave you fulfilled and strong

Just turn to the Lord Almighty
He is always there for you
There is no trial in this world
He will not carry you through

Finally, be strong in the Lord and in his mighty power.

Ephesians 6:10

Anyone who does wrong will be repaid for his wrong, and there is no favoritism.

Colossians 3:25

but those who hope in the Lord will renew their strength. They will soar on wings like eagles; they will run and not grow weary, they will walk and not be faint.

Isaiah 40:31

JULY 31

Sometimes I feel so much joy
Too much joy to contain
Give me the courage to share
And bring Your kingdom gain

Remind me not everyone knows
I must not hold this in
Put my feet upon the path
Where You will have me begin

For we cannot help speaking about what we have
seen and heard."

Acts 4:20

But you will receive power when the Holy Spirit
comes on you; and you will be my witnesses in
Jerusalem, and in all Judea and Samaria, and to
the ends of the earth."

Acts 1:8

Clap your hands, all you nations; shout to God
with cries of joy.

Psalm 47:1

AUGUST 1

Don't let me grow stagnant
Like the water in a pond
Run Your living waters through me
Meeting expectations and beyond

Let the good news flow
From me like a waterfall
Until everyone hears Your word
And Your wave carries us all

Whoever believes in me, as the Scripture has said, streams of living water will flow from within him."

John 7:38

He said to me: "It is done. I am the Alpha and the Omega, the Beginning and the End. To him who is thirsty I will give to drink without cost from the spring of the water of life.

Revelation 21:6

For I will pour water on the thirsty land, and streams on the dry ground; I will pour out my Spirit on your offspring, and my blessing on your descendants.

Isaiah 44:3

AUGUST 2

We always talk about God's love
Have you ever thought about His patience
Knowing we sin daily
It's part of our very essence

Telling a child the same thing
Over and over again
Makes us feel exasperated
How does our God not get wore thin

Bear in mind that our Lord's patience means salvation, just as our dear brother Paul also wrote you with the wisdom that God gave him.
2 Peter 3:15

Be completely humble and gentle; be patient, bearing with one another in love.
Ephesians 4:2

Rend your heart and not your garments. Return to the Lord your God, for he is gracious and compassionate, slow to anger and abounding in love, and he relents from sending calamity.
Joel 2:13

AUGUST 3

It's unbelievable that God never gives up
He has one big crazy flock of sheep
With His unending love and grace
I'm thankful He is willing to keep

He always loves and cares for me
Picks me up no matter how far I fall
Making me want to change and be better
God has room above for us all

In my Father's house are many rooms; if it were
not so, I would have told you. I am going there
to prepare a place for you.

John 14:2

"Do not be afraid, little flock, for your Father has
been pleased to give you the kingdom.

Luke 12:32

For you were like sheep going astray, but now
you have returned to the Shepherd and Overseer
of your souls.

1 Peter 2:25

AUGUST 4

Little moments compile a lifetime
And they are full of ups and downs
The moment that should matter the most
Is when we accept Jesus and His crown

From that moment we are made new
Yet our life will still face trials
But knowing the place of our eternal home
Beats the old moments by miles

and to put on the new self, created to be like God in true righteousness and holiness.
Ephesians 4:24

My times are in your hands; deliver me from my enemies and from those who pursue me.
Psalm 31:15

who will transform our lowly body to be like his glorious body, by the power that enables him even to subject all things to himself.
Philippians 3:21 (ESV)

AUGUST 5

Mercy, what a beautiful thing to share
Maybe to this we could commit
What a blessing it would be beyond compare
If our world had more of it

We should try to be more like our Father
And show more people mercy and love
Reach out and make a difference to one another
Then we will receive riches from above

But because of his great love for us, God, who is
rich in mercy,
Ephesians 2:4

because judgement without mercy will be shown
to anyone who has not been merciful. Mercy tri-
umphs over judgement!
James 2:13

Be merciful, just as your Father is merciful.
Luke 6:36

AUGUST 6

If there is one thing in this world
You could pick to make a change
Would you make that change happen
If you felt it was within your range

Well if you pray for God's will
And He has led you to this part
If you have faith as big as a mustard seed
He will give you the tools to start

Then I heard the voice of the Lord saying,
"Whom shall I send? And who will go for us?"
And I said, "Here am I. Send me!"
Isaiah 6:8

The apostles said to the Lord, "Increase our
faith!"
Luke 17:5

With this in mind, we constantly pray for you,
that our God may count you worthy of his call-
ing, and that by his power he may fulfill every
good purpose of yours and every act prompted
by your faith.
2 Thessalonians 1:11

AUGUST 7

What is fear to you
Being scared of a certain thing
Or worrying about your future
Of what tomorrow will bring

Are you scared of doing something
Or fear something left undone
The only thing you should fear
Is not accepting God's only Son

But the eyes of the Lord are on those who fear
him, on those whose hope is in his unfailing love,
Psalm 33:18

and teaching them to obey everything I have
commanded you. And surely I am with you
always, to the very end of the age."
Matthew 28:20

Fear of man will prove to be a snare, but whoever
trusts in the Lord is kept safe.
Proverbs 29:25

AUGUST 8

There's always tomorrow
Seems to be a common theme
Tomorrow is not promised
And may not be as it seems

For if the Lord returned today
And this world came to an end
Will you be lifted up to heaven
Or left in a hell wrapped in sin

Do not boast about tomorrow, for you do not
know what a day may bring forth.
Proverbs 27:1

Why, you do not even know what will happen
tomorrow. What is your life? You are a mist that
appears for a little while and then vanishes.
James 4:14

He who overcomes will inherit all this, and I will
be his God and he will be my son. But the cow-
ardly, the unbelieving, the vile, the murderers,
the sexually immoral, those who practice magic
arts, the idolaters and all liars—their place will
be in the fiery lake of burning sulfur. This is the
second death."
Revelation 21:7–8

AUGUST 9

How can you think about God's goodness
And not be shaken to the core
To be saved while still a sinner
But wait, there is so much more

He loves us and protects us
Gives us unending mercy and grace
Forgives us all our trespasses
And provides our eternal resting place

But God demonstrates his own love for us in this:
While we were still sinners, Christ died for us.
Romans 5:8

Taste and see that the Lord is good; blessed is the
man who takes refuge in him.
Psalm 34:8

And he said, "I will make all my goodness pass
before you and will proclaim before you my name
'The Lord.' And I will be gracious to whom I will
be gracious, and will show mercy on whom I will
show mercy.
Exodus 33:19 (ESV)

AUGUST 10

God gave us this world to live in
But to be of this world we are not
By our faith and good deeds
We are to build up our eternal spot

So do not bother with earthly treasure
Or succumb to desires of this world
Seek only to please our Father
And let the opinion of man be furled

For everything in the world—the cravings of sinful man, the lust of his eyes and the boasting of what he has and does—comes not from the Father but from the world.
1 John 2:16

But store up for yourselves treasures in heaven, where moth and rust do not destroy, and where thieves do not break in and steal.
Matthew 6:20

How can you believe if you accept praise from one another, yet make no effort to obtain the praise that comes from the only God?
John 5:44

AUGUST 11

Why do we feel the need to compare
Can we not just be content
Comparing leads to negative thoughts
It is not time well spent

We don't know others needs
Or how they made their gain
The pettiness that comes from it
Is not worth all the pain

"You shall not covet your neighbor's house. You shall not covet your neighbor's wife, or his manservant or maidservant, his ox or donkey, or anything that belongs to your neighbor."
Exodus 20:17

It is these who cause divisions, worldly people, devoid of the Spirit.
Jude 1:19 (ESV)

For where you have envy and selfish ambition, there you find disorder and every evil practice.
James 3:16

AUGUST 12

When you think you have nothing
Just know someone has less
And if you think you have chaos
Just know there's a bigger mess

When you think you have it bad
Someone out there has it worse
God will meet all of your needs
If you accept Him and converse

And my God will meet all your needs according
to his glorious riches in Christ Jesus.
Philippians 4:19

"Ask and it will be given to you; seek and you will
find; knock and the door will be opened to you.
Matthew 7:7

For our light and momentary troubles are achiev-
ing for us an eternal glory that far outweighs
them all.
2 Corinthians 4:17

I bet everything alive
Has something we should admire
Or maybe something we could learn
If we only desire

Take the life of a turtle
Long, and he is diligent and slow
Which is something we wish for
And how in Christ we should grow

Even the stork in the sky knows her appointed seasons, and the dove, the swift and the thrush observe the time of their migration. But my people do not know the requirements of the Lord.
Jeremiah 8:7

Go to the ant, you sluggard; consider its ways and be wise!
Proverbs 6:6

"But ask the animals, and they will teach you, or the birds of the air, and they will tell you;
Job 12:7

There are things that happen in life
By someone else or our own hand
That are devastating to say the least
And definitely not as we planned

What happened is not who you are
It is something that happened to you
God's love for you does not falter
Turn to Him, He will carry you through

O Israel, put your hope in the Lord, for with the Lord is unfailing love and with him is full redemption.

Psalm 130:7

You hear, O Lord, the desire of the afflicted; you encourage them, and you listen to their cry, defending the fatherless and the oppressed, in order that man, who is of the earth, may terrify no more.

Psalm 10:17–18

Even to your old age and gray hairs I am he, I am he who will sustain you. I have made you and I will carry you; I will sustain you and I will rescue you.

Isaiah 46:4

Has someone ever done something for you
That absolutely blew your mind away
You were so thankful and overwhelmed
With no idea what to do or say

Take that feeling and apply it to this
God gave His only Son to die for you
A gift of eternal life given freely by grace
Knowing this, what are you going to do

But I, with a song of thanksgiving, will sacrifice to you. What I have vowed I will make good. Salvation comes from the Lord."
Jonah 2:9

"For God so loved the world that he gave his one and only Son, that whoever believes in him shall not perish but have eternal life.
John 3:16

He himself bore our sins in his body on the tree, so that we might die to sins and live for righteousness; by his wounds you have been healed.
1 Peter 2:24

AUGUST 16

We are given so many opportunities
To set things in our lives right
Yet we keep putting it off
Not knowing why we put up a fight

Time is not on your side
Today may be your last chance
Put the devil in his place and run to God
It's time for you to change your stance

But thanks be to God! He gives us the victory through our Lord Jesus Christ.
                    1 Corinthians 15:57

As a cloud vanishes and is gone, so he who goes down to the grave does not return.
                    Job 7:9

So you also must be ready, because the Son of Man will come at an hour when you do not expect him.
                    Matthew 24:44

AUGUST 17

Are they really that nice
Have you ever heard yourself ask
Well yes, they probably are
And it's not that hard of a task

Ask God into your heart
Surround yourself with His word
Dive deep into His love for you
And the same niceness from you will be heard

He will yet fill your mouth with laughter and
your lips with shouts of joy.
Job 8:21

Let your conversation be always full of grace, sea-
soned with salt, so that you may know how to
answer everyone.
Colossians 4:6

God is not unjust; he will not forget your work
and the love you have shown him as you have
helped his people and continue to help them.
Hebrews 6:10

AUGUST 18

I fail in some way every day
But that does not break my spirit
For God is a song in my heart
And I can't wait for you to hear it

So I ask for forgiveness
And I go on about my day
Because the love and grace of God
Picks me up, wipes me off and lights my way

Keep me from deceitful ways; be gracious to me through your law.

Psalm 119:29

This is love: not that we loved God, but that he loved us and sent his Son as an atoning sacrifice for our sins.

1 John 4:10

I will praise you, O Lord, with all my heart; I will tell of all your wonders.

Psalm 9:1

AUGUST 19

I am so very blessed
By the glory of Your love
The peace You give me
Fits me like a glove

I am thankful for Your presence
And Your eternal gift
My heart is full of praise
From You may I not drift

Do not cast me from your presence or take your
Holy Spirit from me.
Psalm 51:11

For the wages of sin is death, but the gift of God
is eternal life in Christ Jesus our Lord.
Romans 6:23

And let the peace of Christ rule in your hearts, to
which indeed you were called in one body. And
be thankful.
Colossians 3:15 (ESV)

AUGUST 20

Refresh me Lord while I sleep
Like the outside morning dew
Watch over me in pleasant dreams
And make me feel brand new

Have the cares of the day drift away
Bring me restful slumber
Plant thoughts softly in my mind
That no man can put asunder

when you lie down, you will not be afraid; when
you lie down, your sleep will be sweet.
Proverbs 3:24

At this I awoke and looked around. My sleep had
been pleasant to me.
Jeremiah 31:26

In a dream, in a vision of the night, when deep
sleep falls on men as they slumber in their beds,
Job 33:15

AUGUST 21

Being brave is different
To each and every one
You may have to save a life
I might have to speak to someone

So let us lift each other up
No matter how big the feat
Give glory to God for the courage
To overcome and defeat

Be strong, and let your heart take courage, all you who wait for the Lord!
Psalm 31:24 (ESV)

David also said to Solomon his son, "Be strong and courageous, and do the work. Do not be afraid or discouraged, for the Lord God, my God, is with you. He will not fail you or forsake you until all the work for the service of the temple of the Lord is finished.
1 Chronicles 28:20

Be strong and let us fight bravely for our people and the cities of our God. The Lord will do what is good in his sight."
2 Samuel 10:12

AUGUST 22

Who needs the fountain of youth
When you have eternal life
Your beauty deepens and grows
With each coming joy or strife

So embrace life as it comes
Do not be saddened by aging
Fill your years with Jesus
His ways are quite engaging

but whoever drinks the water I give him will never thirst. Indeed, the water I give him will become in him a spring of water welling up to eternal life."

John 4:14

Flee the evil desires of youth, and pursue righteousness, faith, love and peace, along with those who call on the Lord out of a pure heart.

2 Timothy 2:22

Gray hair is a crown of splendor; it is attained by a righteous life.

Proverbs 16:31

AUGUST 23

God is the most important accessory
You can adorn yourself with each day
So be sure you always take Him
When you go upon your way

He loves to sing with you in the car
And say hello to the passer by
To be a constant prayer in your mind
Or a hug for a friend while they cry

Your beauty should not come from outward adornment, such as braided hair and the wearing of gold jewelry and fine clothes. Instead, it should be that of your inner self, the unfading beauty of a gentle and quiet spirit, which is of great worth in God's sight.
1 Peter 3:3–4

"I am the vine; you are the branches. If a man remains in me and I in him, he will bear much fruit; apart from me you can do nothing.
John 15:5

I have set the Lord always before me. Because he is at my right hand, I will not be shaken.
Psalm 16:8

AUGUST 24

We always try to multitask
So we can get more things done
And although the tasks might be complete
They aren't 100 percent on each one

Let's apply this to life and God
And see what ends up on our lip
For you can't live in fear and in faith
Or simultaneously speak of worry and worship

He is before all things, and in him all things hold together.

Colossians 1:17

There is no fear in love. But perfect love drives out fear, because fear has to do with punishment. The one who fears is not made perfect in love.

1 John 4:18

The Lord says: "These people come near to me with their mouth and honor me with their lips, but their hearts are far from me. Their worship of me is made up only of rules taught by men.

Isaiah 29:13

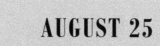

AUGUST 25

If one more door closes in my life
I don't know what I will do
I feel I have done all I can
But have I fully trusted in You

Please give me the patience to be still
And the courage to give You control
The strength to live my life
With Your hands guiding my soul

Find rest, O my soul, in God alone; my hope comes from him.

Psalm 62:5

Better is the end of a thing than its beginning, and the patient in spirit is better than the proud in spirit.

Ecclesiastes 7:8 (ESV)

The Lord will fight for you; you need only to be still."

Exodus 14:14

AUGUST 26

When we were born
We had many things to learn
And as we grew up
Trust we had to earn

When we were born again
The cycle was restarted
For we were made new
From our old selves we parted

Like newborn babies, crave pure spiritual milk,
so that by it you may grow up in your salvation,
1 Peter 2:2

When I was a child, I talked like a child, I thought
like a child, I reasoned like a child. When I
became a man, I put childish ways behind me.
1 Corinthians 13:11

and have put on the new self, which is being
renewed in knowledge in the image of its Creator.
Colossians 3:10

AUGUST 27

Becoming a Christian
Doesn't mean you can't have fun
And it doesn't mean you can't have things
While you follow the Holy One

It means be kind and compassionate
Share with those in need
Don't do certain things in excess
And cut out things of bad seed

For you have been born again, not of perishable seed, but of imperishable, through the living and enduring word of God.

1 Peter 1:23

Therefore let us keep the Festival, not with the old yeast, the yeast of malice and wickedness, but with bread without yeast, the bread of sincerity and truth.

1 Corinthians 5:8

It teaches us to say "No" to ungodliness and worldly passions, and to live self-controlled, upright and godly lives in this present age,

Titus 2:12

AUGUST 28

When you have an ailment
And you feel like a burden
Those caring for you feel differently
And help because they love I am certain

For we all have different needs
And different abilities to share
So shoo those bad thoughts away
Knowing we do it because we care

He who gives to the poor will lack nothing, but he who closes his eyes to them receives many curses.

Proverbs 28:27

We who are strong ought to bear with the failings of the weak and not to please ourselves.

Romans 15:1

And the prayer offered in faith will make the sick person well; the Lord will raise him up. If he has sinned, he will be forgiven.

James 5:15

AUGUST 29

When you face a mental illness
You may harbor feelings of guilt or shame
Please put those thoughts to rest
For He and we love you just the same

We need to face it together
Just as with any chronic disease
Stop worrying about what others think
Treat, move forward, and give it to God please

Those who look to him are radiant; their faces are
never covered with shame.

Psalm 34:5

It always protects, always trusts, always hopes,
always perseveres.

1 Corinthians 13:7

Dear friends, since God so loved us, we also
ought to love one another.

1 John 4:11

AUGUST 30

You ever love someone so much
You could squeeze them until they pop
That is how much God loves us
Plus even more over the top

What a wonderful thing
To feel so fully loved
Remember how good it feels also
When reciprocated without being shoved

In this way, love is made complete among us so that we will have confidence on the day of judgement, because in this world we are like him.
1 John 4:17

The Lord appeared to us in the past, saying: "I have loved you with an everlasting love; I have drawn you with loving-kindness.
Jeremiah 31:3

Know therefore that the Lord your God is God; he is the faithful God, keeping his covenant of love to a thousand generations of those who love him and keep his commands.
Deuteronomy 7:9

AUGUST 31

You can lead a horse to water
But you can't make them drink
You can tell them everything you know
But you don't know what they think

You can show them how to live right
But you don't know what they will do
You must introduce them to God
But what happens next is not up to you

All a man's ways seem right to him, but the Lord weighs the heart.

Proverbs 21:2

"I the Lord search the heart and examine the mind, to reward a man according to his conduct, according to what his deeds deserve."

Jeremiah 17:10

Blessed are the pure in heart, for they will see God.

Matthew 5:8

SEPTEMBER 1

We don't have to know to know
The details aren't important
We need only have faith in God
Following Him should be a constant

God knows the plan for us
We just need to trust in Him
And know where our heart lies
Any other path is too grim

equip you with everything good for doing his will, and may he work in us what is pleasing to him, through Jesus Christ, to whom be glory for ever and ever. Amen.
Hebrews 13:21

Then he said to them all: "If anyone would come after me, he must deny himself and take up his cross daily and follow me.
Luke 9:23

Whether you turn to the right or to the left, your ears will hear a voice behind you, saying, "This is the way; walk in it."
Isaiah 30:21

SEPTEMBER 2

Have you ever stopped to think about
All the ways you have been blessed
The many answered prayers you have
That you were able to put to rest

Once a prayer seems answered
We quickly move on to another
Remember to always be thankful
For what was given by the Good Father

"The Lord bless you and keep you; the Lord make
his face shine upon you and be gracious to you;
Numbers 6:24-25

May he grant you your heart's desire and fulfill
all your plans!
Psalm 20:4 (ESV)

Therefore I tell you, whatever you ask for in
prayer, believe that you have received it, and it
will be yours.
Mark 11:24

SEPTEMBER 3

Your love covers me like a blanket
On a cold winter's day
It keeps me warm and safe
Thank you is all I know to say

You bring me comfort and peace
In a chaotic and crazy world
You are my solid rock
Where so many stones are hurled

the Lord turn his face toward you and give you peace."
Numbers 6:26

He is the Rock, his works are perfect, and all his ways are just. A faithful God who does no wrong, upright and just is he.
Deuteronomy 32:4

Praise be to the Lord, for he showed his wonderful love to me when I was in a besieged city.
Psalm 31:21

SEPTEMBER 4

If someone says I love you once
And then they are mean the rest of the day
What do you remember the most
When on your pillow your head you do lay

You can't have it both ways
And this is not what true love is
Fix the problem with the right solution
And become a faithful child of His

The Lord is the strength of his people; he is the saving refuge of his anointed.
Psalm 28:8 (ESV)

I call to the Lord, who is worthy of praise, and I am saved from my enemies.
2 Samuel 22:4

For such people are not serving our Lord Christ, but their own appetites. By smooth talk and flattery they deceive the minds of naïve people.
Romans 16:18

SEPTEMBER 5

No greater love has he
Then to lay down their life for you
Which is exactly what Jesus did
To take away our sin and make us new

Thank you for loving me so
And opening up eternity to me
The joy and peace You bring
I will rejoice in for the world to see

For Christ died for sins once for all, the righteous for the unrighteous, to bring you to God. He was put to death in the body but made alive by the Spirit,

1 Peter 3:18

Greater love has no one than this, that he lay down his life for his friends.

John 15:13

My soul will boast in the Lord; let the afflicted hear and rejoice.

Psalm 34:2

SEPTEMBER 6

I wish I could bundle up this feeling
And put it in a bottle
It would be so popular
Probably fly off the shelf full throttle

Instead I have a better offer
And you can feel this way for free
Accept Jesus into your heart
This is for all not just for me

You have filled my heart with greater joy than
when their grain and new wine abound.
Psalm 4:7

and the ransomed of the Lord will return. They
will enter Zion with singing; everlasting joy will
crown their heads. Gladness and joy will overtake
them, and sorrow and sighing will flee away.
Isaiah 35:10

for, "Everyone who calls on the name of the Lord
will be saved."
Romans 10:13

SEPTEMBER 7

How come when we get in trouble
We look for someone else to blame
It's no-one's fault but our own
Everyone else should be treated the same

It's not the person giving discipline
Or how they found out
Our God gives discipline and justice
And we deserve it no doubt

The Lord loves righteousness and justice; the earth is full of his unfailing love.
Psalm 33:5

This only have I found: God made mankind upright, but men have gone in search of many schemes."
Ecclesiastes 7:29

Do not be deceived: God cannot be mocked. A man reaps what he sows.
Galatians 6:7

SEPTEMBER 8

When we overcome something
That seems insurmountable at times
We must join up with God
And our victory feels sublime

Yet once we have won the battle
We cannot think we are done
For the good works are not finished
Until we are called home by the Holy One

For the Lord your God is the one who goes with you to fight for you against your enemies to give you victory."
Deuteronomy 20:4

But thanks be to God! He gives us the victory through our Lord Jesus Christ.
1 Corinthians 15:57

being confident of this, that he who began a good work in you will carry it on to completion until the day of Christ Jesus.
Philippians 1:6

Although salvation is an individual act
Once saved you are no longer meant to be alone
For together we make up the body of Christ
And as that body we carry His throne

Your individual walk is important
So you can be a healthy part of the body
Together we make everything better
And represent Him humbly without being gaudy

So then, just as you received Christ Jesus as Lord, continue to live in him,
Colossians 2:6

From him the whole body, joined and held together by every supporting ligament, grows and builds itself up in love, as each part does its work.
Ephesians 4:16

shepherd the flock of God that is among you, exercising oversight, not under compulsion, but willingly, as God would have you; not for shameful gain, but eagerly;
1 Peter 5:2 (ESV)

SEPTEMBER 10

When God draws you near
He will call upon your name
It may only happen once
Your eternity is no game

Will you come to Him in tears
Or be frozen in your tracks
Remember if He never calls again
There are no take backs

"No one can come to me unless the Father who sent me draws him, and I will raise him up at the last day.

John 6:44

If anyone's name was not found written in the book of life, he was thrown into the lake of fire.

Revelation 20:15

but whoever denies me before men, I also will deny before my Father who is in heaven.

Matthew 10:33 (ESV)

SEPTEMBER 11

What will you do today
To show someone you care
That their life really matters
And they are worthy beyond compare

You might be the light,
The only light they see
So share the love of God
And help someone be free

to speak evil of no one, to avoid quarreling, to be gentle, and to show perfect courtesy toward all people.

Titus 3:2 (ESV)

Having purified your souls by your obedience to the truth for a sincere brotherly love, love one another earnestly from a pure heart,

1 Peter 1:22 (ESV)

In the same way, let your light shine before men, that they may see your good deeds and praise your Father in heaven.

Matthew 5:16

SEPTEMBER 12

Missions are not just needed
Halfway around our globe
They are right in front of us
Finding them doesn't take much of a probe

So knowing everyone faces struggles
You don't have to go far to offer aid
Be sure to give the glory to God
And don't make it a parade

There will always be poor people in the land.
Therefore I command you to be openhanded
toward your brothers and toward the poor and
needy in your land.

Deuteronomy 15:11

He who oppresses the poor shows contempt for
their Maker, but whoever is kind to the needy
honors God.

Proverbs 14:31

"Be careful not to do your 'acts of righteousness'
before men, to be seen by them. If you do, you
will have no reward from your Father in heaven.

Matthew 6:1

SEPTEMBER 13

I have such appreciation
For God's never-ending peace
I know whatever the world gives
My trust in Him will not cease

He wants me to be okay
And because of Him I will
My heart is His and His is mine
In His love I am still

The Lord gives strength to his people; the Lord blesses his people with peace.
Psalm 29:11

And the effect of righteousness will be peace, and the result of righteousness, quietness and trust forever.
Isaiah 32:17 (ESV)

But whoever is united with the Lord is one with him in spirit.
1 Corinthians 6:17 (NIV)

SEPTEMBER 14

I am sometimes overwhelmed
By how much God does love
He provides me with refuge
Like the wings of a dove

There is not a step I take
That I am not in His care
He surrounds me always
He is like my air

The Lord will guide you always; he will satisfy your needs in a sun-scorched land and will strengthen your frame. You will be like a well-watered garden, like a spring whose waters never fail.
Isaiah 58:11

He will cover you with his feathers, and under his wings you will find refuge; his faithfulness will be your shield and rampart.
Psalm 91:4

The Spirit of God has made me; the breath of the Almighty gives me life.
Job 33:4

I don't have to be an artist
To paint the perfect picture in my mind
For it's a place of possibility
Where I leave all restrictions behind

It's like a piece of heaven on earth
A place I can always go
And all the creations in there
Only God and I know

Set your minds on things above, not on earthly things.

Colossians 3:2

The mind of sinful man is death, but the mind controlled by the Spirit is life and peace;

Romans 8:6

to be made new in the attitude of your minds;

Ephesians 4:23

SEPTEMBER 16

If you are always looking down
Can you imagine what you miss
There are wonders all around
Please take note of this

The smile of someone as you pass by
Sadness in the eyes of those in need
A blessing meant just for you
Or the opportunity to do a good deed

Do not neglect to show hospitality to strangers, for thereby some have entertained angels unawares.

Hebrews 13:2 (ESV)

Abraham looked up and saw three men standing nearby. When he saw them, he hurried from the entrance of his tent to meet them and bowed low to the ground.

Genesis 18:2

Even a child is known by his actions, by whether his conduct is pure and right.

Proverbs 20:11

SEPTEMBER 17

I will wait for You
For I know You are not finished
Although I don't know Your plan
My faith in You will not be diminished

I will pray and follow You
And be thankful for the time
You graciously give to me
To assure I make the climb

Then he said to them all: "If anyone would come after me, he must deny himself and take up his cross daily and follow me.
Luke 9:23

So do not throw away your confidence; it will be richly rewarded.
Hebrews 10:35

In his heart a man plans his course, but the Lord determines his steps.
Proverbs 16:9

SEPTEMBER 18

A birthday or anniversary
Should be a celebration
The reason why is simple
Shouldn't require elaboration

Just in case you're wondering
What you really need to know
Be thankful for a year of blessings
And another year to grow

For through me your days will be many, and
years will be added to your life.

Proverbs 9:11

And this is my prayer: that your love may abound
more and more in knowledge and depth of
insight,

Philippians 1:9

For we are God's workmanship, created in Christ
Jesus to do good works, which God prepared in
advance for us to do.

Ephesians 2:10

SEPTEMBER 19

Don't forget God's love for you
No matter how long you have to wait
The devil will put many trials in your way
Please do not take the bait

Remain faithful and trust God
He is for you not against
Once His plan comes to fruition
Your blessings will be dispensed

equip you with everything good for doing his will, and may he work in us what is pleasing to him, through Jesus Christ, to whom be glory for ever and ever. Amen.

Hebrews 13:21

Wait for the Lord; be strong and take heart and wait for the Lord.

Psalm 27:14

Yet the Lord longs to be gracious to you; he rises to show you compassion. For the Lord is a God of justice. Blessed are all who wait for him!

Isaiah 30:18

SEPTEMBER 20

Holy Spirit fill me up
Let me be Your vessel
Please consider my heart and soul
A place You can safely nestle

Allow me to carry You
Humbly everywhere I go
Thank you, dear Lamb of God
For washing me white as snow

But the Counselor, the Holy Spirit, whom the Father will send in my name, will teach you all things and will remind you of everything I have said to you.

John 14:26

Cleanse me with hyssop, and I will be clean; wash me, and I will be whiter than snow.

Psalm 51:7

And I will put my Spirit within you, and cause you to walk in my statutes and be careful to obey my rules.

Ezekiel 36:27 (ESV)

SEPTEMBER 21

Why are we so demanding
On a God so gracious and kind
Who do we think we are
We must be out of our mind

Yes if we ask for something
We are promised to receive
If we have faith in His will
Is the part we forget to conceive

"Not everyone who says to me, 'Lord, Lord,' will enter the kingdom of heaven, but only he who does the will of my Father who is in heaven.
Matthew 7:21

"For who has known the mind of the Lord that he may instruct him?" But we have the mind of Christ.
1 Corinthians 2:16

"So I say to you: Ask and it will be given to you; seek and you will find; knock and the door will be opened to you.
Luke 11:9

SEPTEMBER 22

Imagine every desert
In a giant hourglass
It still does not compare
To the love you could let pass

Eternity is much longer
Than that falling sand
Don't let the hourglass run out
Before you take His precious hand

He led you through the vast and dreadful desert, that thirsty and waterless land, with its venomous snakes and scorpions. He brought you water out of hard rock.

Deuteronomy 8:15

How precious to me are your thoughts, O God! How vast is the sum of them! Were I to count them, they would outnumber the grains of sand. When I awake, I am still with you.

Psalm 139:17–18

But everyone who hears these words of mine and does not put them into practice is like a foolish man who built his house on sand.

Matthew 7:26

SEPTEMBER 23

Be mindful of your words
They are mirrors to your heart
To make them both Christ like
We must daily take part

For just when I think
My hearts in a better place
I say something I regret
Leaving me seeking forgiveness and grace

May the words of my mouth and the meditation
of my heart be pleasing in your sight, O Lord, my
Rock and my Redeemer.

Psalm 19:14

The good man brings good things out of the
good stored up in his heart, and the evil man
brings evil things out of the evil stored up in his
heart. For out of the overflow of his heart his
mouth speaks.

Luke 6:45

But I tell you that men will have to give account
on the day of judgement for every careless word
they have spoken.

Matthew 12:36

SEPTEMBER 24

If you want to think better
You need to learn to pray
Because if you are praying for someone
Then you won't have much bad to say

If there is something negative
That has a grip on your inner being
Use the time you think about it with God
And He will change how you are seeing

Finally, brothers, whatever is true, whatever is noble, whatever is right, whatever is pure, whatever is lovely, whatever is admirable—if anything is excellent or praiseworthy—think about such things.

Philippians 4:8

We demolish arguments and every pretension that sets itself up against the knowledge of God, and we take captive every thought to make it obedient to Christ.

2 Corinthians 10:5

Set your minds on things above, not on earthly things.

Colossians 3:2

SEPTEMBER 25

Hugs are a special gift
They lift you up when you are blue
And let someone know you care
Or your appreciation is true

They can make you feel important
A simple expression of love
Even make you feel safe
Wrapped in comfort from above

So he got up and went to his father. "But while he was still a long way off, his father saw him and was filled with compassion for him; he ran to his son, threw his arms around him and kissed him.
Luke 15:20

As a mother comforts her child, so will I comfort you; and you will be comforted over Jerusalem."
Isaiah 66:13

But Esau ran to meet Jacob and embraced him; he threw his arms around his neck and kissed him. And they wept.
Genesis 33:4

When you hurt someone's feelings
It is important to say you are sorry
For you should get no pleasure
And your remorse shouldn't be a safari

So hunt no more for forgiveness
Go openly in love to show you care
Admit you were wrong and pray
A sinner without repentance should beware

Godly sorrow brings repentance that leads to salvation and leaves no regret, but worldly sorrow brings death.

2 Corinthians 7:10

leave your gift there in front of the altar. First go and be reconciled to your brother; then come and offer your gift.

Matthew 5:24

I confess my iniquity; I am troubled by my sin.

Psalm 38:18

SEPTEMBER 27

Each experience we have
Is an opportunity to grow
Be it good or bad
Don't turn it into a show

Guard your tongue and your mind
Being thoughtful in your response
There is always a blessing
When we choose a positive nuance

But he gives us more grace. That is why Scripture says: "God opposes the proud but gives grace to the humble."

James 4:6

Let the wise hear and increase in learning, and the one who understands obtain guidance,

Proverbs 1:5 (ESV)

Not that I have already obtained all this, or have already been made perfect, but I press on to take hold of that for which Christ Jesus took hold of me.

Philippians 3:12

SEPTEMBER 28

No matter how good of life you lead
Or how upright in this world you are
There is only one way to guarantee
Where your eternity will be, by far

It will not be because of good works
But by God's amazing grace
Then you and your good works will be new
Once you make your heart God's dwelling place

he saved us, not because of righteous things we had done, but because of his mercy. He saved us through the washing of rebirth and renewal by the Holy Spirit,

Titus 3:5

For it is by grace you have been saved, through faith—and this not from yourselves, it is the gift of God—not by works, so that no one can boast.

Ephesians 2:8–9

For we hold that one is justified by faith apart from works of the law.

Romans 3:28 (ESV)

SEPTEMBER 29

King of kings, above all other names
My Rock, Redeemer and Savior
There are so many uplifting descriptions
That alone should make you seek His favor

Yes other things are wonderful too
And can go by different names
But none of them died and rose again
There is no other that can make these claims

Salvation is found in no one else, for there is no other name under heaven given to men by which we must be saved."

Acts 4:12

Therefore God exalted him to the highest place and gave him the name that is above every name,

Philippians 2:9

He is not here; he has risen, just as he said. Come and see the place where he lay.

Matthew 28:6

You ever notice darkness runs from light
It will always stir around and leave
And anything remaining in the dark
Can easily trick the eye and deceive

The devil is like the darkness
For he is never what he seems
So let God be the light of your life
And walk in the protection of His beams

For he has rescued us from the dominion of darkness and brought us into the kingdom of the Son he loves,

Colossians 1:13

to open their eyes and turn them from darkness to light, and from the power of Satan to God, so that they may receive forgiveness of sins and a place among those who are sanctified by faith in me.'

Acts 26:18

For you are all children of light, children of the day. We are not of the night or of the darkness.

1 Thessalonians 5:5 (ESV)

OCTOBER 1

If life was a recipe
Then our cookbook should be the bible
And we wonder why we don't rise
When we don't treat its contents viable

We must get all the ingredients
And follow the written directions
If we want to bake up
Into God's finest confections

Jesus answered, "It is written: 'Man does not live on bread alone, but on every word that comes from the mouth of God.'"

Matthew 4:4

He humbled you, causing you to hunger and then feeding you with manna, which neither you nor your fathers had known, to teach you that man does not live on bread alone but on every word that comes from the mouth of the Lord.

Deuteronomy 8:3

for he satisfies the thirsty and fills the hungry with good things.

Psalm 107:9

OCTOBER 2

Growing up we are taught independence
How to take care of things on our own
Is it possible we are leaving out a step
That helps us depend on God when we are grown

We need to add the action of praying
When we are teaching others to grow
So we develop that dependence on God
And to never cease praying is what we know

Train a child in the way he should go, and when he is old he will not turn from it.
Proverbs 22:6

Impress them on your children. Talk about them when you sit at home and when you walk along the road, when you lie down and when you get up.
Deuteronomy 6:7

Fathers, do not exasperate your children; instead, bring them up in the training and instruction of the Lord.
Ephesians 6:4

OCTOBER 3

Just because your testimony
Isn't filled with heartache and doom
Doesn't mean it's not worth sharing
About how God has helped you bloom

For every soul that is saved
Will spend eternity in heaven
It's worth telling what God did for you
Let your words be to them as leaven

It is my pleasure to tell you about the miraculous signs and wonders that the Most High God has performed for me.

Daniel 4:2

How, then, can they call on the one they have not believed in? And how can they believe in the one of whom they have not heard? And how can they hear without someone preaching to them?

Romans 10:14

And this is the testimony: God has given us eternal life, and this life is in his Son.

1 John 5:11

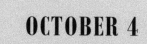

OCTOBER 4

The wonderful sound of chatter
Mixed with laughter all around
Lifts your spirits indeed
And lets happiness abound

Put yourself in situations
Surrounded with joyful noise
Be filled with the gladness it brings
And celebrate the emotions it employs

All the days of the oppressed are wretched, but
the cheerful heart has a continual feast.
Proverbs 15:15

Our mouths were filled with laughter, our
tongues with songs of joy. Then it was said among
the nations, "The Lord has done great things for
them."
Psalm 126:2

For I have derived much joy and comfort from
your love, my brother, because the hearts of the
saints have been refreshed through you.
Philemon 1:7 (ESV)

OCTOBER 5

If you were the painter
Of each sunrise and sunset
Could you always design
Something hard to forget

If that's difficult to imagine
Think of the Almighty Creator
Continually making anew
Never being an imitator

Do you know how the clouds hang poised, those wonders of him who is perfect in knowledge?
Job 37:16

The whole earth is filled with awe at your wonders; where morning dawns, where evening fades, you call forth songs of joy.
Psalm 65:8 (NIV)

Do you not know? Have you not heard? The Lord is the everlasting God, the Creator of the ends of the earth. He will not grow tired or weary, and his understanding no one can fathom.
Isaiah 40:28

OCTOBER 6

Do you think free will costs
And are you willing to pay the price
For we usually know the right choice
Yet choose to ignore our own advice

So when your payment comes due
What you decide to do next is key
You can stay on your path and see how it goes
Or pray for repentance and guidance from Thee

For the sinful nature desires what is contrary to the Spirit, and the Spirit what is contrary to the sinful nature. They are in conflict with each other, so that you do not do what you want.
Galatians 5:17

This day I call heaven and earth as witnesses against you that I have set before you life and death, blessings and curses. Now choose life, so that you and your children may live
Deuteronomy 30:19

Those who oppose him he must gently instruct, in the hope that God will grant them repentance leading them to a knowledge of the truth, and that they will come to their senses and escape from the trap of the devil, who has taken them captive to do his will.
2 Timothy 2:25–26

OCTOBER 7

Have you ever prayed to know
If there is something God wants you to do
And you feel like you understand what He says
Yet you are too scared to follow through

Well if it is truly God's will
And you throw out all inhibition
You can trust God's plan and be blessed
While you work towards doing your mission

By faith Noah, when warned about things not yet seen, reverently prepared an ark to save his family, and by faith he condemned the world and inherited the righteousness that comes by faith.
Hebrews 11:7 (ISV)

Moses answered the people, "Do not be afraid. Stand firm and you will see the deliverance the Lord will bring you today. The Egyptians you see today you will never see again.
Exodus 14:13

If that is how God clothes the grass of the field, which is here today, and tomorrow is thrown into the fire, how much more will he clothe you, O you of little faith!
Luke 12:28

OCTOBER 8

Sometimes when we pray for something
It may not be answered as we want
For we never know what He may bring
We should be thankful and do not taunt

Although we think we know what is best
We cannot see or understand the entire plan
So trust in God to fill in the rest
Because He is our biggest fan

When you ask, you do not receive, because you ask with wrong motives, that you may spend what you get on your pleasures.

James 4:3

I have sought your face with all my heart; be gracious to me according to your promise.

Psalm 119:58

"I am the Lord's servant," Mary answered. "May it be to me as you have said." Then the angel left her.

Luke 1:38

OCTOBER 9

Jesus was the most powerful man
To ever have walked the earth
He could have or do anything He wanted
We should mimic Him for all it's worth

For He never took advantage of anyone
He shared kindness, love and healing all around
Always willing to serve and never sinned
To His Father He stayed humbly bound

For we do not have a high priest who is unable to sympathize with our weaknesses, but we have one who has been tempted in every way, just as we are—yet was without sin.
Hebrews 4:15

For even the Son of Man did not come to be served, but to serve, and to give his life as a ransom for many."
Mark 10:45

The men were amazed and asked, "What kind of man is this? Even the winds and the waves obey him!"
Matthew 8:27

OCTOBER 10

Beware of false teachers
That change God's word
Usually to suit their agenda
The outcome can be absurd

So get to know your bible
Gain the loving knowledge yourself
Take the messages that are wrong
And put them away on a shelf

For the time will come when men will not put up with sound doctrine. Instead, to suit their own desires, they will gather around them a great number of teachers to say what their itching ears want to hear.

2 Timothy 4:3

Dear friends, do not believe every spirit, but test the spirits to see whether they are from God, because many false prophets have gone out into the world.

1 John 4:1

See to it that no one takes you captive through hollow and deceptive philosophy, which depends on human tradition and the basic principles of this world rather than on Christ.

Colossians 2:8

OCTOBER 11

My heart was broken
Something I wanted fell through
I was beside myself
And didn't know what to do

Then I remembered God's promise
I was overcome by His love
And I knew I would be okay
Because of His divine plan from above

Keep your lives free from the love of money and be content with what you have, because God has said, "Never will I leave you; never will I forsake you."

Hebrews 13:5

Humble yourselves, therefore, under God's mighty hand, that he may lift you up in due time.

1 Peter 5:6

Dear friends, now we are children of God, and what we will be has not yet been made known. But we know that when he appears, we shall be like him, for we shall see him as he is.

1 John 3:2

OCTOBER 12

What makes you so bitter
We like to blame others it's true
But the truth lies deeper within
If your bitter, it is because of you

You are the only person
That can control your every thought
Don't let that bitterness settle in
Instead put Jesus in its spot

See to it that no one fails to obtain the grace of God; that no "root of bitterness" springs up and causes trouble, and by it many become defiled;
Hebrews 12:15 (ESV)

"I loathe my very life; therefore I will give free rein to my complaint and speak out in the bitterness of my soul.
Job 10:1

Get rid of all bitterness, rage and anger, brawling and slander, along with every form of malice.
Ephesians 4:31

OCTOBER 13

Picture you as the ocean
And your spirit was your pier
What things do you harbor
Love and kindness or anger and fear

What stays there is up to you
Keeping your waters choppy or calm
Spreading waves of doubt and anger
Or soothing sprays of psalm

for man's anger does not bring about the righ-
teous life that God desires.

James 1:20

They are wild waves of the sea, foaming up their
shame; wandering stars, for whom blackest dark-
ness has been reserved forever.

Jude 1:13

He stilled the storm to a whisper; the waves of
the sea were hushed. They were glad when it grew
calm, and he guided them to their desired haven.

Psalm 107:29–30

OCTOBER 14

Why do we nitpick and judge
When we are meant to lift up
Causing hard feelings or a grudge
Instead of putting love in our cup

Take a moment right now to pray
For strength to set pettiness aside
That you will tear no one down today
And see them humbly without pride

Therefore, rid yourselves of all malice and all deceit, hypocrisy, envy, and slander of every kind.
1 Peter 2:1

Let no corrupting talk come out of your mouths, but only such as is good for building up, as fits the occasion, that it may give grace to those who hear.
Ephesians 4:29 (ESV)

So then let us pursue what makes for peace and for mutual upbuilding.
Romans 14:19 (ESV)

OCTOBER 15

We are all so busy thinking
What do others think of us
Really our concern should be
Are we living right by Jesus

For if we live as He says
Then our actions fall into place
And if someone wishes to judge
It will be at their own disgrace

For it is God's will that by doing good you should
silence the ignorant talk of foolish men.
1 Peter 2:15

When a man's ways are pleasing to the Lord, he
makes even his enemies live at peace with him.
Proverbs 16:7

But the Lord is with me like a mighty warrior;
so my persecutors will stumble and not prevail.
They will fail and be thoroughly disgraced; their
dishonor will never be forgotten.
Jeremiah 20:11

OCTOBER 16

Amongst all the hate in the world
I feel so abundant with love
God please show me how to disperse it
So others obtain the glory above

I am so full I could almost burst
And no longer wish to hold this in
My cup runneth over with Your love
God tell me where You want me to begin

Give, and it will be given to you. A good measure, pressed down, shaken together and running over, will be poured into your lap. For with the measure you use, it will be measured to you."
Luke 6:38

Many are the woes of the wicked, but the Lord's unfailing love surrounds the man who trusts in him.
Psalm 32:10

Mercy, peace and love be yours in abundance.
Jude 1:2

OCTOBER 17

Please speak kindly to those you love
Try not to say things you may regret
It may be the last time you see them
Would the hurt be something you could forget

So if you say something that is hurtful
Don't let the sun set with that on your heart
Say you are sorry and ask their forgiveness
And from this horrible habit depart

"In your anger do not sin": Do not let the sun go down while you are still angry,
Ephesians 4:26

Reckless words pierce like a sword, but the tongue of the wise brings healing.
Proverbs 12:18

Repent, therefore, of this wickedness of yours, and pray to the Lord that, if possible, the intent of your heart may be forgiven you.
Acts 8:22 (ESV)

OCTOBER 18

Do you see others as God sees you
A person to be cherished and loved
Regardless of the mistakes they made
To draw near not pushed and shoved

Someone you only want the best for
Full of hope that they may succeed
That your heart aches when they hurt
And you help when they are in need

Accept one another, then, just as Christ accepted
you, in order to bring praise to God.
Romans 15:7

Be completely humble and gentle; be patient,
bearing with one another in love.
Ephesians 4:2

Ears that hear and eyes that see—the Lord has
made them both.
Proverbs 20:12

OCTOBER 19

What's holding you back
From accepting His call
Are you afraid of failure
That you might stumble or fall

Well the truth is
You more than likely will
It's the end result you get
That is the big deal

though he stumble, he will not fall, for the Lord
upholds him with his hand.
Psalm 37:24

Even youths grow tired and weary, and young
men stumble and fall;
Isaiah 40:30

Some of the wise will stumble, so that they may
be refined, purified and made spotless until
the time of the end, for it will still come at the
appointed time.
Daniel 11:35

OCTOBER 20

Is your world what you want it to be
Does something feel like it is missing
Or maybe you just need a change
Are you always doing and never listening

Let's take the time together to stop
Set everything circling around you aside
Now hear our God calling to you
Lay it at His feet and let Him be your guide

So faith comes from hearing, and hearing through the word of Christ.
Romans 10:17 (ESV)

But he said, "Blessed rather are those who hear the word of God and keep it!"
Luke 11:28 (ESV)

And he said to me, "Son of man, listen carefully and take to heart all the words I speak to you.
Ezekiel 3:10

OCTOBER 21

When you are feeling all alone
My brother, my sister, you are mistaken
Our God is with you, holding you
His love for you will never be shaken

He is always there providing comfort
Lift your loneliness up in prayer
He will never leave you nor forsake you
Reach out and trust He is there

For I am convinced that neither death nor life, neither angels nor demons, neither the present nor the future, nor any powers, neither height nor depth, nor anything else in all creation, will be able to separate us from the love of God that is in Christ Jesus our Lord.

Romans 8:38–39

May the Lord our God be with us as he was with our fathers; may he never leave us nor forsake us.

1 Kings 8:57

Turn to me and be gracious to me, for I am lonely and afflicted.

Psalm 25:16

OCTOBER 22

Are you always trying to justify
What you have said or done
When the only justification that matters
Is the gift given from God's Son

Let me justify my statement
On this your eternity depends
Without the justification of God
The chance of heavenly eternity ends

and are justified by his grace as a gift, through the
redemption that is in Christ Jesus,
Romans 3:24 (ESV)

so that, having been justified by his grace, we
might become heirs having the hope of eternal
life.
Titus 3:7

And that is what some of you were. But you were
washed, you were sanctified, you were justified
in the name of the Lord Jesus Christ and by the
Spirit of our God.
1 Corinthians 6:11

OCTOBER 23

A shattered life isn't ugly
It can be difficult it is true
Yet a wonderful masterpiece
What you make of it is up to you

For the pieces are the color of life
Put together make a beautiful mosaic
And when God binds them with love
It is far more than prosaic

I said, "O Lord, have mercy on me; heal me, for I have sinned against you."
Psalm 41:4

God, pick up the pieces. Put me back together again. You are my praise!
Jeremiah 17:14 (MSG)

Therefore, if anyone is in Christ, he is a new creation; the old has gone, the new has come!
2 Corinthians 5:17

We are all equally important
In the eyes of our Father
Regardless of our place in life
No one is better than the other

We are all given the same promise
And fully encompassed by His grace
Don't let someone belittle you
Nor look down on other's place

There is neither Jew nor Greek, slave nor free, male nor female, for you are all one in Christ Jesus.

Galatians 3:28

Rich and poor have this in common: The Lord is the Maker of them all.

Proverbs 22:2

Then Peter began to speak: "I now realize how true it is that God does not show favoritism

Acts 10:34

OCTOBER 25

It is considered rude in most cultures
To refuse, deny or discard a gift
And when it comes from our God
Our thanks and acceptance also does drift

First, we deny the gift of salvation
And then once we accept this in our heart
We do not seek and use our spiritual gift
Which of our salvation is a big part

Thanks be to God for his indescribable gift!
2 Corinthians 9:15

Follow the way of love and eagerly desire spiritual
gifts, especially the gift of prophecy.
1 Corinthians 14:1

Each one should use whatever gift he has received
to serve others, faithfully administering God's
grace in its various forms.
1 Peter 4:10

If it were within my power
To make you feel better
I would spend every minute of every hour
Sending healing in each letter

If I can love you that much
Imagine the love our God has for you
For we haven't met in gaze or touch
That's just what the power of God can do

Do everything in love.
1 Corinthians 16:14

Dear friends, let us love one another, for love comes from God. Everyone who loves has been born of God and knows God.
1 John 4:7

Now that you have purified yourselves by obeying the truth so that you have sincere love for your brothers, love one another deeply, from the heart.
1 Peter 1:22

OCTOBER 27

You are to serve until your last breath
For you are never too old to share
He asks you to give all you can
And the glories you receive will not compare

So don't think you are beyond serving
Although your age may change what you can do
Don't ever be through with serving God
Because He is never through serving you

They will still bear fruit in old age, they will stay fresh and green,

Psalm 92:14

Therefore we do not lose heart. Though outwardly we are wasting away, yet inwardly we are being renewed day by day.

2 Corinthians 4:16

Moses was 120 years old when he died. His eye was undimmed, and his vigor unabated.

Deuteronomy 34:7 (ESV)

OCTOBER 28

Is your faith in need of irrigation
Have you neglected to cultivate
There is but one way to end the drought
To give you living water He does wait

Don't take too long to receive the water
Your faith will become a dry thirsty land
His word will provide that nourishment
Our God will provide you His hand

But the seed on good soil stands for those with a noble and good heart, who hear the word, retain it, and by persevering produce a crop.
Luke 8:15

"But blessed is the man who trusts in the Lord, whose confidence is in him. He will be like a tree planted by the water that sends out its roots by the stream. It does not fear when heat comes; its leaves are always green. It has no worries in a year of drought and never fails to bear fruit."
Jeremiah 17:7–8

The righteous will flourish like a palm tree, they will grow like a cedar of Lebanon;
Psalm 92:12

OCTOBER 29

The past is behind you for a reason
Leave it there and move forward to grow
Remember all that it has taught you
Pray on what to keep and what to let go

And when the past knocks on your door
Tell it the old you is dead and gone
You can hold me captive no more
For to our Savior I have been drawn

For you have spent enough time in the past doing what pagans choose to do—living in debauchery, lust, drunkenness, orgies, carousing and detestable idolatry.

1 Peter 4:3

Jesus replied, "No one who puts his hand to the plow and looks back is fit for service in the kingdom of God."

Luke 9:62

Brothers, I do not consider myself yet to have taken hold of it. But one thing I do: Forgetting what is behind and straining toward what is ahead, I press on toward the goal to win the prize for which God has called me heavenward in Christ Jesus.

Philippians 3:13–14

OCTOBER 30

We were made to worship together
God meant us to live in unity
Not just meaning to be at peace
But to be equally yoked with our company

So get up and go to church
Come together in our common desire
To share in love, praise and worship
And draw closer to the God we admire

Let us not give up meeting together, as some are in the habit of doing, but let us encourage one another—and all the more as you see the Day approaching.

Hebrews 10:25

Let the word of Christ dwell in you richly as you teach and admonish one another with all wisdom, and as you sing psalms, hymns and spiritual songs with gratitude in your hearts to God.

Colossians 3:16

They devoted themselves to the apostles' teaching and to the fellowship, to the breaking of bread and to prayer.

Acts 2:42

If you are wrong can you admit it
Do you buy only the nicest things
Looking down on others as you do this
Gloating on the joy it brings

Are you feeling irreplaceable at work
Thinking you do everything better than others
Maybe your pride is running over
While putting yourself before God and your brothers

For everything in the world—the cravings of sinful man, the lust of his eyes and the boasting of what he has and does—comes not from the Father but from the world.

1 John 2:16

Do nothing out of selfish ambition or vain conceit, but in humility consider others better than yourselves.

Philippians 2:3

The pride of your heart has deceived you, you who live in the clefts of the rocks and make your home on the heights, you who say to yourself, 'Who can bring me down to the ground?'

Obadiah 1:3

NOVEMBER 1

God is here for you
Through every up and down
He will lift you up
And share with you His crown

So call upon Him first
When going through good or bad
For comfort if you need it
And giving glory when you are glad

This is good, and pleases God our Savior,
1 Timothy 2:3

You will be a crown of splendor in the Lord's hand, a royal diadem in the hand of your God.
Isaiah 62:3

The Lord is my strength and my shield; my heart trusts in him, and I am helped. My heart leaps for joy and I will give thanks to him in song.
Psalms 28:7

NOVEMBER 2

I love the peace God brings
He makes my spirit feel at ease
With these feelings my heart sings
I bow in praise on my knees

Knowing I can face each day
His comfort overtakes my mind
Ready for anything that comes my way
Leaving all of those fears behind

May your unfailing love be my comfort, according to your promise to your servant.

Psalm 119:76

God is our refuge and strength, an ever-present help in trouble.

Psalm 46:1

When all the people of Israel saw the fire come down and the glory of the Lord on the temple, they bowed down with their faces to the ground on the pavement and worshiped and gave thanks to the Lord, saying, "For he is good, for his steadfast love endures forever."

2 Chronicles 7:3 (ESV)

NOVEMBER 3

When I see someone full of sadness
My heart goes out with a prayer
Lord let them receive your comfort
And tell me how to show them I care

My eyes tear up and my heart aches
I can't imagine the depth of their pain
Don't let them go with that hurt
Share God's love so peace they will gain

Rejoice with those who rejoice; mourn with those who mourn.

Romans 12:15

who comforts us in all our troubles, so that we can comfort those in any trouble with the comfort we ourselves have received from God.

2 Corinthians 1:4

But a Samaritan, as he journeyed, came to where he was, and when he saw him, he had compassion.

Luke 10:33 (ESV)

NOVEMBER 4

Of all the things I can't answer
I understand God loves me
There is not a moment I am alone
And there is nothing He cannot see

This leaves me feeling so blessed
Knowing there is nothing I can't defeat
I pray for the opportunity and courage
To share this with others I meet

Because of the Lord's great love we are not con-
sumed, for his compassions never fail.
Lamentations 3:22

The eternal God is your refuge, and underneath
are the everlasting arms. He will drive out your
enemy before you, saying, 'Destroy him!'
Deuteronomy 33:27

and teaching them to obey everything I have
commanded you. And surely I am with you
always, to the very end of the age."
Matthew 28:20

NOVEMBER 5

Look at the beauty in a storm
Nothing smells better then fresh rain
The sound of thunder barreling across the sky
Bolts of lightning are anything but plain

It awakens all of our senses
And oh, the new growth that does follow
When you go through a storm of your own
Embrace it, don't let it leave you hollow

When you pass through the waters, I will be with
you; and when you pass through the rivers, they
will not sweep over you. When you walk through
the fire, you will not be burned; the flames will
not set you ablaze.
                              Isaiah 43:2

The Lord is good, a refuge in times of trouble.
He cares for those who trust in him,
                              Nahum 1:7

And after you have suffered a little while, the
God of all grace, who has called you to his eter-
nal glory in Christ, will himself restore, confirm,
strengthen, and establish you.
                              1 Peter 5:10 (ESV)

Without being under a rain cloud
I couldn't ever dance in the rain
If I never lost anything
I may not understand when I gain

Could I feel joy when something was fixed
When nothing in my life was broken
Would I know the importance of this all
If to me His words were never spoken

I pray also that the eyes of your heart may be enlightened in order that you may know the hope to which he has called you, the riches of his glorious inheritance in the saints,

Ephesians 1:18

Then he opened their minds so they could understand the Scriptures.

Luke 24:45

The god of this age has blinded the minds of unbelievers, so that they cannot see the light of the gospel of the glory of Christ, who is the image of God.

2 Corinthians 4:4

NOVEMBER 7

You are the potter, Lord
And I am Your clay
Mold me and shape me
To make a beautiful display

So that You will be glorified
In Your wonderous creation
Glaze me in pure white
Draw me to Your nation

Yet, O Lord, you are our Father. We are the clay, you are the potter; we are all the work of your hand.

Isaiah 64:8

But we have this treasure in jars of clay to show that this all-surpassing power is from God and not from us.

2 Corinthians 4:7

"O house of Israel, can I not do with you as this potter does?" declares the Lord. "Like clay in the hand of the potter, so are you in my hand, O house of Israel.

Jeremiah 18:6

NOVEMBER 8

Are you holding back when you worship
To raise your hand in praise you're at the brink
God doesn't hold back glorifying you
He isn't wondering what the angels think

So lift your hands when you are led
Don't hold back when you sing Him praise
Give to God as freely as He gives to you
Maybe it's time to change your ways

I will praise you as long as I live, and in your
name I will lift up my hands.
Psalm 63:4

My lips will shout for joy when I sing praise to
you—I, whom you have redeemed.
Psalm 71:23

And those he predestined, he also called; those
he called, he also justified; those he justified, he
also glorified.
Romans 8:30

We were made to walk on water
When it is something Jesus commands
Our faith will keep us afloat
Reach out and take His precious hands

This is how we are overcomers
Able to get the impossible done
By faith not sight it is accomplished
Conquering your feat with the Almighty One

"Come," he said. Then Peter got down out of the
boat, walked on the water and came toward Jesus.
Matthew 14:29

For nothing is impossible with God."
Luke 1:37

The Sovereign Lord is my strength; he makes my
feet like the feet of a deer, he enables me to go on
the heights.
Habakkuk 3:19

NOVEMBER 10

Why do people that are Christian
Talk about someone behind their back
That's a way to ruin your witness
And bring Christians under attack

The truth is being a Christian
Doesn't keep us from making mistakes
Growth, guilt, repentance and forgiveness
In our Father's love is the difference it makes

for all have sinned and fall short of the glory of
God,
Romans 3:23

Keep me from deceitful ways; be gracious to me
through your law.
Psalm 119:29

Repent, then, and turn to God, so that your sins
may be wiped out, that times of refreshing may
come from the Lord,
Acts 3:19

NOVEMBER 11

As Christians we are to be Christ like
Although we try, we are not perfect
What happens once we make a mistake
Is the difference we hope to project

Have faith that God still loves you
Humbly confess and ask to be forgiven
Do your best not to do it again
Show by the Holy Spirit you are driven

I have declared to both Jews and Greeks that they must turn to God in repentance and have faith in our Lord Jesus.

Acts 20:21

Peter replied, "Repent and be baptized, every one of you, in the name of Jesus Christ for the forgiveness of your sins. And you will receive the gift of the Holy Spirit.

Acts 2:38

if my people, who are called by my name, will humble themselves and pray and seek my face and turn from their wicked ways, then will I hear from heaven and will forgive their sin and will heal their land.

2 Chronicles 7:14

Amazing is how much love He has
Amazing He sent His Son to die for me
Amazing the amount of comfort He gives
Amazing that through Him I am free

Amazing amount of mercy He offers
Amazing from the lost we were found
Amazing that He made us His own
Amazing grace how it does abound

See what amazing love the Father has given us!
Because of it, we are called children of God. And
that's what we really are! The world doesn't know
us because it didn't know him.
1 John 3:1 (NIRV)

I have been crucified with Christ. It is no longer
I who live, but Christ who lives in me. And the
life I now live in the flesh I live by faith in the Son
of God, who loved me and gave himself for me.
Galatians 2:20 (ESV)

For from his fullness we have all received, grace
upon grace.
John 1:16 (ESV)

NOVEMBER 13

Think of all the feelings
Our Lord does evoke
It can bring you to tears
Without a word being spoke

If it feels that way here
Then just try to comprehend
The amazement once in heaven
Once your time on earth does end

With joy you will draw water from the wells of salvation.

Isaiah 12:3

Everyone was amazed and gave praise to God. They were filled with awe and said, "We have seen remarkable things today."

Luke 5:26

that their hearts may be encouraged, being knit together in love, to reach all the riches of full assurance of understanding and the knowledge of God's mystery, which is Christ,

Colossians 2:2 (ESV)

NOVEMBER 14

The smile on my face is sincere
It comes from an inner joy
Provided by God our Father
That the Holy Spirit does deploy

Even if there is a moment
That I might feel a little down
The joy within does not flee
Smiles feel much better than a frown

Those who look to him are radiant; their faces are
never covered with shame.
Psalm 34:5

A happy heart makes the face cheerful, but heart-
ache crushes the spirit.
Proverbs 15:13

And the ransomed of the Lord shall return and
come to Zion with singing; everlasting joy shall
be upon their heads; they shall obtain gladness
and joy, and sorrow and sighing shall flee away.
Isaiah 51:11 (ESV)

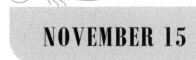

NOVEMBER 15

We could never give enough thanks
To you Lord for Your special gift
Sometimes we feel so unworthy
With Your words those thoughts lift

Not only thank you for what You did
With the opportunity that provided
But for loving me beyond measure
And in me being delighted

Let them give thanks to the Lord for his unfailing love and his wonderful deeds for men,
Psalm 107:8

For it is by grace you have been saved, through faith—and this not from yourselves, it is the gift of God—
Ephesians 2:8

For the Lord takes delight in his people; he crowns the humble with salvation.
Psalm 149:4

NOVEMBER 16

We always try to think of things
To secure our future and improve our life
Like saving money or buying a home
Maybe looking for a husband or a wife

All of these things are blessings
But the most important change to make
Is answering the call of our Savior
By giving Him your heart to take

For where your treasure is, there your heart will
be also.

Matthew 6:21

Wealth is worthless in the day of wrath, but righ-
teousness delivers from death.

Proverbs 11:4

He called you to this through our gospel, that
you might share in the glory of our Lord Jesus
Christ.

2 Thessalonians 2:14

If you want to change your life
Here is an awesome easy solution
Accept Jesus in your heart
Call it a new life resolution!

It would be longer than weeks or years
That this decision will affect
Your salvation and eternal home
Is what you will collect

And this is eternal life, that they know you, the only true God, and Jesus Christ whom you have sent.

John 17:3 (ESV)

But now that you have been set free from sin and have become slaves to God, the benefit you reap leads to holiness, and the result is eternal life.

Romans 6:22

receiving as the result of your faith, the salvation of your souls.

1 Peter 1:9 (AMP)

NOVEMBER 18

We must change the way we think
Because sin is not only words or action
For even our thoughts are sin
And usually our thoughts gain traction

With Christ we must retrain our mind
To be filled with what is good
By delving daily into His word
And praying it's His word we understood

Then, after desire has conceived, it gives birth to
sin; and sin, when it is full-grown, gives birth to
death.

James 1:15

Those who live according to the sinful nature
have their minds set on what that nature desires;
but those who live in accordance with the Spirit
have their minds set on what the Spirit desires.

Romans 8:5

to be made new in the attitude of your minds;

Ephesians 4:23

NOVEMBER 19

God didn't make us above other creatures
So we would always worry and fret
For in His word He assures us
That our basic needs would be met

He created us in His image
So we may bring Him worship and praise
Loving Him boldly as His children
To share that love the rest of our days

Look at the birds of the air; they do not sow or reap or store away in barns, and yet your heavenly Father feeds them. Are you not much more valuable than they?

Matthew 6:26

Then God said, "Let us make man in our image, in our likeness, and let them rule over the fish of the sea and the birds of the air, over the livestock, over all the earth, and over all the creatures that move along the ground."

Genesis 1:26

the people whom I formed for myself that they might declare my praise.

Isaiah 43:21 (ESV)

NOVEMBER 20

Time with those you love
Is precious time indeed
Make memories while you can
Call on those when you need

Fill the time with goodness
Overflowing with love and laughter
For once they are in heaven
Those memories you will be after

A wise son brings joy to his father, but a foolish man despises his mother.
Proverbs 15:20

How good and pleasant it is when brothers live together in unity!
Psalm 133:1

The memory of the righteous will be a blessing, but the name of the wicked will rot.
Proverbs 10:7

NOVEMBER 21

Draw near to God our Father
In the midst of your hurt and pain
He will surround you in comfort
Causing your anguish to wane

His love for you is endless
The desire to help is the same
Pour out your heart to Him
Then refill it with His holy name

Let us then with confidence draw near to the throne of grace, that we may receive mercy and find grace to help in time of need.

Hebrews 4:16 (ESV)

He heals the brokenhearted and binds up their wounds.

Psalm 147:3

Praise be to the God and Father of our Lord Jesus Christ, the Father of compassion and the God of all comfort,

2 Corinthians 1:3

Do those around you know you love them
Are they confident in how much you care
Telling them occasionally isn't enough
You should be constantly making them aware

Always tell them that you love them
Remember actions speak louder than your word
Share the good news of our Father
This will be the best thing they have ever heard

If anyone does not provide for his relatives, and especially for his immediate family, he has denied the faith and is worse than an unbeliever.

1 Timothy 5:8

Impress them on your children. Talk about them when you sit at home and when you walk along the road, when you lie down and when you get up.

Deuteronomy 6:7

And over all these virtues put on love, which binds them all together in perfect unity.

Colossians 3:14

NOVEMBER 23

Why do you go on vacation
To leave all your cares behind
Be surrounded by people you love
Renew your spirit and clear your mind

Well I'm on vacation every Sunday
I leave church fulfilled and refreshed
My worries are left at the door
And with the fellowship I am blessed

What then, brothers? When you come together, each one has a hymn, a lesson, a revelation, a tongue, or an interpretation. Let all things be done for building up.
1 Corinthians 14:26 (ESV)

Praise the Lord! I will give thanks to the Lord with my whole heart, in the company of the upright, in the congregation.
Psalm 111:1 (ESV)

For I will satisfy the weary soul, and every languishing soul I will replenish."
Jeremiah 31:25 (ESV)

NOVEMBER 24

When you are going through things in life
And you feel like there is no end
Keep the faith and trust in God
Believe its completion He will send

For if we lose faith and give up
We grow tired and stop searching
Imagine the changes in our history
If our forefathers just stopped marching

But as for you, be strong and do not give up, for
your work will be rewarded."
2 Chronicles 15:7

And let us not grow weary of doing good, for in due
season we will reap, if we do not give up.
Galatians 6:9 (ESV)

By faith the walls of Jericho fell, after the people
had marched around them for seven days.
Hebrews 11:30

Faith was made to bring you through
Giving you hope when all else is lost
Always know the end result will be
For your good and worth the cost

So when hard times call your name
Put all your worry and doubt aside
Get on your knees and pray
Letting God lift you up from inside

for it is God who works in you to will and to act according to his good purpose.
Philippians 2:13

And hope does not disappoint us, because God has poured out his love into our hearts by the Holy Spirit, whom he has given us.
Romans 5:5

For our light and momentary troubles are achieving for us an eternal glory that far outweighs them all.
2 Corinthians 4:17

NOVEMBER 26

The only fight you need to be in
Is the one to lay your battle down
Humbly giving them to the Almighty
Because in this He is renown

He fights against the wicked
Protecting you against your enemy
For the righteous He wins battles
In Christ you can claim victory

With God we will gain the victory, and he will trample down our enemies.

Psalm 108:13

The Lord will fight for you; you need only to be still."

Exodus 14:14

Though I walk in the midst of trouble, you preserve my life; you stretch out your hand against the wrath of my enemies, and your right hand delivers me.

Psalm 138:7 (ESV)

NOVEMBER 27

Remember the story of Moses
How God was always by his side
All the miracles He performed
And the deliverance He did provide

Just as God was with Moses
He is with me and you
Never leaving our side
By faith He will see us through

No one will be able to stand up against you all the days of your life. As I was with Moses, so I will be with you; I will never leave you nor forsake you.

Joshua 1:5

And I will ask the Father, and he will give you another Counselor to be with you forever—

John 14:16

"The virgin will be with child and will give birth to a son, and they will call him Immanuel"—which means, "God with us."

Matthew 1:23

NOVEMBER 28

Are you the bowl or the spoon
Careful of this you should be
The bowl is a vessel to stir in
While the spoon stirs up disharmony

As the bowl, be a good container
Only pouring out what is good
As the spoon try not to divide
Pretending you are misunderstood

As for a person who stirs up division, after warning him once and then twice, have nothing more to do with him,

Titus 3:10 (ESV)

For such people are not serving our Lord Christ, but their own appetites. By smooth talk and flattery they deceive the minds of naïve people.

Romans 16:18

How good and pleasant it is when brothers live together in unity!

Psalm 133:1

NOVEMBER 29

Out of all the names you can be called
The most significant is God calling you His own
There is no better place to be in life
No greater love could ever be known

I am so thankful that He saw me
And I came to Him when He did call
I became a child of our God
There is room in His arms for all

"I will be a Father to you, and you will be my sons and daughters, says the Lord Almighty."
2 Corinthians 6:18

But now thus says the Lord, he who created you, O Jacob, he who formed you, O Israel: "Fear not, for I have redeemed you; I have called you by name, you are mine.
Isaiah 43:1 (ESV)

So you are no longer a slave, but a son; and since you are a son, God has made you also an heir.
Galatians 4:7

NOVEMBER 30

The dream of many is
To be loved as you are
If you know where to look
You don't have to go far

God seeks the broken
Those laden with sin
Come as you are
He will take you in

Come to me, all who labor and are heavy laden, and I will give you rest.
Matthew 11:28 (ESV)

"Come now, let us reason together," says the Lord. "Though your sins are like scarlet, they shall be as white as snow; though they are red as crimson, they shall be like wool.
Isaiah 1:18

On hearing this, Jesus said to them, "It is not the healthy who need a doctor, but the sick. I have not come to call the righteous, but sinners."
Mark 2:17

DECEMBER 1

Are you the one that has gone astray
Wondering around lost looking for your way
Our God is the one that on this day
Leaves the ninety-nine saving one from prey

You might think how does this weigh
Leaving you not knowing what to say
But for you your sin He will slay
By asking Him to save you when you pray

"What do you think? If a man owns a hundred sheep, and one of them wanders away, will he not leave the ninety-nine on the hills and go to look for the one that wandered off?
Matthew 18:12

I tell you that in the same way there will be more rejoicing in heaven over one sinner who repents than over ninety-nine righteous persons who do not need to repent.
Luke 15:7

I have strayed like a lost sheep. Seek your servant, for I have not forgotten your commands.
Psalm 119:176

DECEMBER 2

Popeye had his spinach
Samson had his hair
Where does your strength lie
Speculate if you dare

My strength lies in Jesus
He is my steady source
Thinking it's from somewhere else
Really throws me off course

Look to the Lord and his strength; seek his face
always.

1 Chronicles 16:11

Surely God is my salvation; I will trust and not
be afraid. The Lord, the Lord, is my strength and
my song; he has become my salvation."

Isaiah 12:2

The Lord is the strength of his people, a fortress
of salvation for his anointed one.

Psalm 28:8

DECEMBER 3

Have you been saved and baptized
For one goes with the other
Yet you must be saved and believe
Don't be confused on this my brother

Being saved is asking Jesus in your heart
Obtaining eternal life and sins being forgiven
Baptism shows profession of your faith
A cleansing of sins and the Holy Spirit being given

That if you confess with your mouth, "Jesus is Lord," and believe in your heart that God raised him from the dead, you will be saved.
Romans 10:9

Whoever believes and is baptized will be saved, but whoever does not believe will be condemned.
Mark 16:16

Peter replied, "Repent and be baptized, every one of you, in the name of Jesus Christ for the forgiveness of your sins. And you will receive the gift of the Holy Spirit.
Acts 2:38

DECEMBER 4

Lord please give me strength
For so much I need to be strong
To leave my past behind
Or admit when I am wrong

Strength to do what is right
To daily follow You
Ignore my earthly desires
And embrace me as new

I thank Christ Jesus our Lord, who has given me strength, that he considered me faithful, appointing me to his service.
1 Timothy 1:12

But you, Lord! Don't be far away! You are my strength! Come quick and help me!
Psalm 22:19 (CEB)

That is why, for Christ's sake, I delight in weaknesses, in insults, in hardships, in persecutions, in difficulties. For when I am weak, then I am strong.
2 Corinthians 12:10

DECEMBER 5

What is being brave mean to you
Getting out of bed to face the day
Spending time with someone new
Letting go of things being done a certain way

Trusting your kids will be fine on their own
Understanding you will always be okay
Being brave is knowing your never alone
And the Lord is there for you come what may

For I am the Lord, your God, who takes hold of your right hand and says to you. Do not fear; I will help you.

Isaiah 41:13

I sought the Lord, and he answered me; he delivered me from all my fears.

Psalm 34:4

And blessed is she who believed that there would be a fulfillment of what was spoken to her from the Lord."

Luke 1:45 (ESV)

DECEMBER 6

Let us pray for revival
Revival of the joy in our heart
Renew in me the fire
That I had at salvations start

Fill me up with Your spirit
Until within it does overflow
Then spark in me the desire
To share this wherever I go

Will you not revive us again, that your people
may rejoice in you?

Psalm 85:6

Repent, then, and turn to God, so that your sins
may be wiped out, that times of refreshing may
come from the Lord,

Acts 3:19

for it is light that makes everything visible. This
is why it is said: "Wake up, O sleeper, rise from
the dead, and Christ will shine on you."

Ephesians 5:14

DECEMBER 7

Would you serve a half-cooked meal
Or wash your clothes but not dry
Maybe do half your job at work
And just let a newborn cry

Typically the things that we do
Are done all the way or 100 percent
We should be doing the same for God
Being lukewarm is not how we were meant

Out of the same mouth come praise and cursing.
My brothers, this should not be.
James 3:10

So, because you are lukewarm, and neither hot
nor cold, I will spit you out of my mouth.
Revelation 3:16 (ESV)

They claim to know God, but by their actions
they deny him. They are detestable, disobedient
and unfit for doing anything good.
Titus 1:16

Let Your grace fall on me
Like a fresh shower of morning rain
So I may grow in Your love
That Your sacrifice was not in vane

May I soak up each precious drop
As if it were the blood of the Lamb
Singing praises to the Lord above
Thankful to the Great I Am

Sow for yourselves righteousness, reap the fruit of unfailing love, and break up your unplowed ground; for it is time to seek the Lord, until he comes and showers righteousness on you.
Hosea 10:12

"You heavens above, rain down righteousness; let the clouds shower it down. Let the earth open wide, let salvation spring up, let righteousness grow with it; I, the Lord, have created it.
Isaiah 45:8

He will be like rain falling on a mown field, like showers watering the earth.
Psalm 72:6

DECEMBER 9

In the arms of love
What a wonderful place to be
That is how I feel
Spending time with Thee

Everything fades away
When my mind fills with You
There is nothing I can't be
With a God so true

Know therefore that the Lord your God is God;
he is the faithful God, keeping his covenant of
love to a thousand generations of those who love
him and keep his commands.

Deuteronomy 7:9

and to know this love that surpasses knowledge—
that you may be filled to the measure of all the
fullness of God.

Ephesians 3:19

Now this is eternal life: that they may know you,
the only true God, and Jesus Christ, whom you
have sent.

John 17:3

DECEMBER 10

Do you know how blessed you are
Take a look at the world all around
There is so much desperation
Yet with God your peace is found

He transcends the problems you face
Applying contentment to your circumstance
Be thankful His love endures
You are not blessed by mere chance

May God himself, the God of peace, sanctify you through and through. May your whole spirit, soul and body be kept blameless at the coming of our Lord Jesus Christ.
1 Thessalonians 5:23

The world and its desires pass away, but the man who does the will of God lives forever.
1 John 2:17

Praise the Lord, O my soul, and forget not all his benefits—
Psalm 103:2

People think when they come to Christ
They have to give up way too much
Isn't your soul worth more
Than using that excuse as a crutch

The fun in your earthly treasures
You may feel cannot be replaced
But the joy in knowing our Lord
Far exceeds a soul eternally misplaced

If I had not come and spoken to them, they would not be guilty of sin. Now, however, they have no excuse for their sin.
John 15:22

"But they all alike began to make excuses. The first said, 'I have just bought a field, and I must go and see it. Please excuse me.'
Luke 14:18

Then my soul will rejoice in the Lord and delight in his salvation.
Psalm 35:9

DECEMBER 12

People grow with nourishment
For body and spirit it is the same
Obtaining proper growth seems easy
Once you learn how to play the game

The body is common knowledge
Regular exercise and a healthy diet
Spiritual is a daily walk with Jesus
It is a beautiful thing; you should try it!

So whether you eat or drink or whatever you do, do it all for the glory of God.
1 Corinthians 10:31

Jesus answered, "It is written: 'Man does not live on bread alone, but on every word that comes from the mouth of God.'"
Matthew 4:4

Everyone who competes in the games goes into strict training. They do it to get a crown that will not last; but we do it to get a crown that will last forever.
1 Corinthians 9:25

What is the foundation
Of which your life is built
Are your walls plumb and true
Or are you at full tilt

It's never too late to rebuild
Bow down at the Carpenter's feet
He will build you in the way
Of a life plumb and complete

For no one can lay any foundation other than the one already laid, which is Jesus Christ.
1 Corinthians 3:11

But the one who hears my words and does not put them into practice is like a man who built a house on the ground without a foundation. The moment the torrent struck that house, it collapsed and its destruction was complete."
Luke 6:49

And in him you too are being built together to become a dwelling in which God lives by his Spirit.
Ephesians 2:22

DECEMBER 14

When you pray to our God
Come to Him in praise and need
Pray to our Father boldly
With expectation of His will to heed

If you pray for something
Trust our God has heard
Believe the answer will come
For it is promised in His word

Ask boldly, believingly, without a second thought. People who "worry their prayers" are like wind-whipped waves.

James 1:6 (MSG)

This is the confidence we have in approaching God: that if we ask anything according to his will, he hears us.

1 John 5:14

Then you will call upon me and come and pray to me, and I will listen to you.

Jeremiah 29:12

DECEMBER 15

How many days do you go
Without speaking to those you love
Are you sure to make it daily
Do you do the same for God above

He wants to be in our lives
Every moment of every day
And to love God as we should
Daily to Him we must pray

You will pray to him, and he will hear you, and you will fulfill your vows.
Job 22:27

Very early in the morning, while it was still dark, Jesus got up, left the house and went off to a solitary place, where he prayed.
Mark 1:35

pray continually;
1 Thessalonians 5:17

DECEMBER 16

Help me not take God for granted
Make Him more than a check on my list
Let me sing praises to His name
And my desire to serve persist

May I spend time with You in love
Giving You thanks without demands
Relish with You these moments
Like a bride and groom holding hands

So then, my friends, because of God's great mercy to us I appeal to you: Offer yourselves as a living sacrifice to God, dedicated to his service and pleasing to him. This is the true worship that you should offer.

Romans 12:1 (GNT)

And they did not do as we expected, but they gave themselves first to the Lord and then to us in keeping with God's will.

2 Corinthians 8:5

Let us rejoice and be glad and give him glory! For the wedding of the Lamb has come, and his bride has made herself ready.

Revelation 19:7

Every day you come to me
It doesn't matter where I go
However I try to avoid you
It is a given you will show

Although you hunt me down
Sometimes even having my consent
My God is bigger than you
And rescues me when I repent

All of us have been sinful; even our best actions are filthy through and through. Because of our sins we are like leaves that wither and are blown away by the wind.

Isaiah 64:6 (GNT)

If we claim to be without sin, we deceive ourselves and the truth is not in us.

1 John 1:8

He who conceals his sins does not prosper, but whoever confesses and renounces them finds mercy.

Proverbs 28:13

DECEMBER 18

As I grow deeper in my faith
Understanding more of His word
Putting others before myself
Seems less and less absurd

I praise them more for their success
And pray more for their path
I hope for their deliverance
Bringing them more in His joy than wrath

Nobody should seek his own good, but the good
of others.

1 Corinthians 10:24

Each of us should please his neighbor for his
good, to build him up.

Romans 15:2

If you really keep the royal law found in Scripture,
"Love your neighbor as yourself," you are doing
right.

James 2:8

DECEMBER 19

Half empty or half full
How would you describe your heart
If you want to fill it up
Here is the perfect place to start

Open your heart to Jesus
Let Him pour His love in
When you pour it out to others
He will refill you again and again

Keep your heart with all vigilance, for from it flow the springs of life.
Proverbs 4:23 (ESV)

The goal of this command is love, which comes from a pure heart and a good conscience and a sincere faith.
1 Timothy 1:5

and to know this love that surpasses knowledge—that you may be filled to the measure of all the fullness of God.
Ephesians 3:19

DECEMBER 20

You know in your heart
When you have crossed the line
By denying our God
Not leaving that one thing behind

Instead of forging ahead
Like you're doing nothing wrong
Listen to the Holy Spirit
In your weakness become strong

If we deliberately keep on sinning after we have received the knowledge of the truth, no sacrifice for sins is left,
Hebrews 10:26

So whoever knows the right thing to do and fails to do it, for him it is sin.
James 4:17 (ESV)

Here is a trustworthy saying that deserves full acceptance: Christ Jesus came into the world to save sinners—of whom I am the worst.
1 Timothy 1:15

DECEMBER 21

Our God is a God of mercy
Although you can't see Him face to face
He is with you every step you take
In this earthly life we race

Let His mercy sprinkle down
In a kind word or an embrace
Where grace and compassion are found
Showing us security in our place

But for that very reason I was shown mercy so that in me, the worst of sinners, Christ Jesus might display his unlimited patience as an example for those who would believe on him and receive eternal life.

1 Timothy 1:16

Answer me when I call to you, O my righteous God. Give me relief from my distress; be merciful to me and hear my prayer.

Psalm 4:1

Grace, mercy and peace from God the Father and from Jesus Christ, the Father's Son, will be with us in truth and love.

2 John 1:3

DECEMBER 22

Not only is there power in His name
He shares His power every day
Giving the power of forgiveness
And power over what we do and say

God provides the power to make choices
And the power to push through our troubles
Without Him I feel powerless
With Him my power more than doubles

Be kind and compassionate to one another, forgiving each other, just as in Christ God forgave you.
> Ephesians 4:32

You, my brothers, were called to be free. But do not use your freedom to indulge the sinful nature; rather, serve one another in love.
> Galatians 5:13

For the kingdom of God is not a matter of talk but of power.
> 1 Corinthians 4:20

DECEMBER 23

God made us the salt of the earth
So we may season those we meet
By enhancing the flavor of life
Not with self-righteous conceit

Show them a taste of God's love
That they may know that it is good
May your saltiness never turn bland
Or ever be misunderstood

"Salt is good, but if it loses its saltiness, how can you make it salty again? Have salt in yourselves, and be at peace with each other."
Mark 9:50

Let your conversation be always full of grace, seasoned with salt, so that you may know how to answer everyone.
Colossians 4:6

now that you have tasted that the Lord is good.
1 Peter 2:3

DECEMBER 24

When we pray for healing
For the mentally or physically ill
Realize it comes in many forms
Including how well we can deal

Their symptoms may improve
They could completely subside
Possibly even passing on
How it occurs is God's will to decide

"See now that I myself am He! There is no god besides me. I put to death and I bring to life, I have wounded and I will heal, and no one can deliver out of my hand.
Deuteronomy 32:39

Dear friend, I pray that you may enjoy good health and that all may go well with you, even as your soul is getting along well.
3 John 1:2

Be joyful in hope, patient in affliction, faithful in prayer.
Romans 12:12

DECEMBER 25

Has there ever been such a story
Than the one of our Lord and Savior
How can you believe in His exixtence
But not in His miraculous behavior

I trust they go hand in hand
As do salvation, heaven and eternity
Please look deeper if you are unsure
May He lift the veil so you can see

And without faith it is impossible to please God, because anyone who comes to him must believe that he exists and that he rewards those who earnestly seek him.

Hebrews 11:6

Beyond all question, the mystery of godliness is great: He appeared in a body, was vindicated by the Spirit, was seen by angels, was preached among the nations, was believed on in the world, was taken up in glory.

1 Timothy 3:16

Bur wherever anyone turns to the Lord, the veil is taken away.

2 Corinthians 3:16

DECEMBER 26

We all need discipline
It's an important part of love
Teaching us right from wrong
Even coming from God above

Pay attention to all your teachings
Love and discipline go hand in hand
Whether you are giving or receiving
Be mindful of the reprimand

No discipline seems pleasant at the time, but
painful. Later on, however, it produces a harvest
of righteousness and peace for those who have
been trained by it.

Hebrews 12:11

"Blessed is the man whom God corrects; so do
not despise the discipline of the Almighty.

Job 5:17

Those whom I love I rebuke and discipline. So be
earnest, and repent.

Revelation 3:19

DECEMBER 27

Being made new in your salvation
Doesn't mean bad habits disappear
Your desire for change increases
As you decrease, this is clear

So don't be upset you are not perfect
For this you will never be
Never give up your efforts
Daily to be more like Thee

He must increase, but I must decrease."
John 3:30 (ESV)

There is not a righteous man on earth who does
what is right and never sins.
Ecclesiastes 7:20

and to put on the new self, created to be like God
in true righteousness and holiness.
Ephesians 4:24

Always be the same person
Wherever it is you may go
Don't come to your house of worship
Just to put on a show

Continually being Christ like
Is a full-time endeavor
Acting different due to surroundings
Truly is not very clever

Dear children, do not let anyone lead you astray. He who does what is right is righteous, just as he is righteous.

1 John 3:7

In the same way, on the outside you appear to people as righteous but on the inside you are full of hypocrisy and wickedness.

Matthew 23:28

If anyone considers himself religious and yet does not keep a tight rein on his tongue, he deceives himself and his religion is worthless.

James 1:26

You know when you finish a project
The gratification that you feel
Is that how God is with us
When we learn to live in His will

Or is it once we are in heaven
When He actually celebrates
Letting His pride and joy shine
As we pass through those pearly gates

This is good, and pleases God our Savior,
1 Timothy 2:3

I tell you that in the same way there will be more rejoicing in heaven over one sinner who repents than over ninety-nine righteous persons who do not need to repent.
Luke 15:7

For this son of mine was dead and is alive again; he was lost and is found.' So they began to celebrate.
Luke 15:24

DECEMBER 30

When you see something wrong
Knowing what to do can be a struggle
Should you say anything about it
Or be quiet, our mind does juggle

So at that moment we should pray
And follow where the spirit leads
Don't do anything for personal gain
Keeping in mind the other's needs

Brothers, if someone is caught in a sin, you who are spiritual should restore him gently. But watch yourself, or you also may be tempted.
Galatians 6:1

remember this: Whoever turns a sinner from the error of his way will save him from death and cover over a multitude of sins.
James 5:20

So watch yourselves. "If your brother sins, rebuke him, and if he repents, forgive him.
Luke 17:3

DECEMBER 31

The joy from serving the Lord
Is a pretty remarkable thing
When you follow the path He reveals
Blessings in abundance it does bring

So when our God calls you
To use the gift He blessed you with
Find your joy in the passion you share
"It's better to give" is not a myth

In everything I did, I showed you that by this kind of hard work we must help the weak, remembering the words the Lord Jesus himself said: 'It is more blessed to give than to receive.'"
Acts 20:35

You have made known to me the path of life; you will fill me with joy in your presence, with eternal pleasures at your right hand.
Psalm 16:11

There are different kinds of working, but the same God works all of them in all men.
1 Corinthians 12:6

ABOUT THE AUTHOR

Traci Britt is no stranger to struggles in life. Not only facing the typical daily things we all face, she has faced the loss of a grandson, a niece and nephew unexpectedly in a short period of time. She also lost her parents shortly thereafter. Being a mom of a blended family of seven provides struggles as well. Then you add some of the kids struggles of drug addiction, incarceration and mental illness you would think there was no room for joy. These are not the only things that define her! There are many blessings in her life including a wonderful husband, children, grandchildren and extended family! But what provides her the inner joy, strength, and ability to face these struggles? She knows the source of her strength, peace, and comfort comes from Jesus Christ! She chose to trust God through it all, to turn to Him for love, comfort and direction! She and her children are overcomers and give all the glory to God. It takes a daily walk with Jesus to grow, and she hopes to continue to grow in His love every day! She was moved to find her spiritual gift and through that journey was led to write this devotional. Her hopes are to help you start or improve your walk with Jesus so you too can know His love for you. Find a legacy worthy of leaving your children, an unshakable and unfailing love for Jesus Christ that brings eternal life!

CPSIA information can be obtained
at www.ICGtesting.com
Printed in the USA
LVHW040808050820
662303LV00001B/88

9 781098 037475